welcome to

THE KOP ANNUAL 2012

KENNY is big news in the Kop Annual this time around.

This was the year the King returned to Anfield and we've celebrated by giving our 2012 edition a tartan theme. Och aye de noo about you, but we think it looks great. I'm sure fellow Scottish new boys Steve Clarke and Charlie Adam love it too. And Jocky.

One of Kenny's first jobs as boss was making wee Andy Carroll feel at home and we've followed the pair's babysitting adventures. We're sure you'll like it, you'll like it, you'll la-la-la-like it.

Elsewhere, we ask 'Whose ground is it anyway' with a quiz to test even the most travelled of Kopites, we pay tribute to Luis Suarez's special kind of magic and find out what Richard Keys and Andy Gray got up to after being caught offside by Sky.

The eighth edition of the Kop Annual also includes regular features from the Kop Mole, LFCBay, Spotted and the best Summer Challenge 5s from 2011 (Kenny shows how it's done below), and there is, shockingly, many a dig aimed at our rivals along the way.

Of course, we couldn't let the opportunity pass without paying tribute to Fernando Torres' first year at his new club. There's many a masterpiece to savour in his Chelsea gallery.

For those unfamiliar with the ahem, genius that is The Kop Annual, it is produced by the makers of the monthly unofficial Kop Magazine. It's all about taking a light-hearted look at our wonderful game.

Every year we take some of The Kop's best bits and mix in loads of brand new features to produce an 84-page glossy extravaganza that we predict you are reading right now.

We also have a Twitter page – @TheKopMagazine – that has more followers than the amount of deadwood shifted by Kenny, Damien Comolli and FSG last summer, and that's saying something.

So welcome to the Kop Annual 2012 and if we don't make you laugh then our special money-back guarantee still applies. That can be found on page 85.

© Published in Great Britain in 2011 by Trinity Mirror Sport Media, PO Box 48, Old Hall Street, Liverpool L69 3EB.

ISBN: 9781906802875

Photographic credits: Trinity Mirror, PA Pics. Illustrations: Peter King.
Writing: Chris McLoughlin. Design/editing: Michael McGuinness, Lee Ashun, Zoe Bevan,
Graham Helliwell, Michael Perry

Craig Bellamy completed the summer arrivals on transfer deadline day and is back in the swing of things at Anfield. With promising signings Jose Enrique and Sebastian Coates also joining in the window, it was par for the course from Kenny to get us back on track after seasons of mediocre buys

THE KOP ANNUAL 2012

CONTENTS

THEY'RE ONLY ON LOAN*

* but Joe and Alberto can stay where they are...

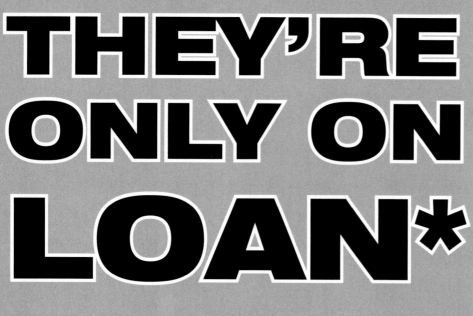

THE LORD OF THE RINGS
THE RETURN OF THE KING

DVD
VIDEO

REMASTERED EDITION

5

Jamie Carragher's 666th appearance in May put him second in our all-time charts behind only Ian Callaghan. Ray Clemence had been in joint second with Emlyn Hughes, but couldn't keeper his place as Carra marches towards 700 in 2011/12

REVEALED: THE HAIR TRANSPLANTS ROONEY REJECTED

With his dazzling good looks, sleek, toned body and a personality and wit only Stephen Fry can match it's a mystery that Wayne Rooney hasn't acquired the media darling status that David Beckham enjoys. But the Rooneys have worked out why. The problem has been the eloquent striker's hairline. It's so obvious. Coleen, sorry Wayne, has sought to rectify the issue by having a hair transplant. The modelling contracts should come rolling in. The KOP lifts the lid on the new hairstyles Rooney said no to...

1. THE CHARLTON SWEEP-OVER: ONLY COSTS A FEW BOB

2. GIGGS CHEST HAIR: A LITTLE MATTED BUT IMOGEN HOW GOOD THIS COULD LOOK

3. THE SCHOLES HAMSTER: FOR THE RETIRING TYPE WHO CAN MAKE A RASH DECISION

4. THE RATBOY WEAVE WITH FREE LIGHTWEIGHT FACIAL HAIR

HE WASN'T THE ONLY ONE THOUGH...

BEFORE

AFTER

Clayton Blackmore

FORMER Manchester United left-back Clayton Blackmore had a reputation as a fearsome hard man on the pitch, but it's hair to say he lost it after this revelation.

Blackmore's thinning thatch bothered him so much he's also had a hair transplant and is now delighted with the results.

"It's really hard to have any hairstyle when you're balding," United's Under-15s coach told the Daily Mirror. "It really bothered me.

"Tracey (his wife) was very supportive. Although she had no problem with my baldness she understood it would make me feel better.

"It slowly started to grow but all of a sudden the person in the mirror had an awful lot more hair! Some might say it's vain, but I think we've all got a little bit of vanity in us."

Clayton Blackmore? Vain? And here's us thinking his permanent orange tan was natural.

The best of SPOTTED

Mark Wright walking past the Ann Summers shop in Liverpool One.

Kenny Dalglish in the main bar area at Formby Hall golf club.

Pepe Reina, dressed in his fluorescent yellow training gear, kindly stopping in his silver Porsche to let a female driver out on to Mill Lane in heavy traffic.

John W Henry in The Cavern, Mathew Street.

Mikel Arteta coming out of San Carlo, Castle Street, with an older looking woman dressed in a horrendous leopard-print fur coat.

Alan Kennedy chatting with Kenny Dalglish at The Academy in Kirkby.

Pub landlord Al Murray eating a plate of clams in J Sheeky Fish & Seafood Restaurant, Covent Garden.

Peter Stringfellow getting into a Smart Car in Covent Garden.

James Corden on the ale in the Sun and 13 Cantons pub, Soho.

Danielle Lloyd having a meal in San Carlo, Castle Street the day afterthe New Year's Day win against Bolton.

Jonah Lomu stood outside the Hilton, Liverpool One, in a vest despite it snowing heavily a couple of days after January's Blackburn game.

ITV news presenter Nicolas Owen getting on a train to Birmingham at Lime Street station.

Roy Hodgson going for a stroll with his wife in Sefton Park on the day Kenny Dalglish was appointed Liverpool manager.

Craig Johnson on a catamaran moored off the coast of Nassau in the Bahamas on the day of the Manchester United v Liverpool cup match.

BBC F1 presenter Jake Humphrey at the Birmingham NEC for the Autosport International show.

Sammy Lee carrying a giant

Buttering them up: Henry and Werner like their sarnies

picture frame into Melwood.

Professor Robert Winston walking past Costa Coffee on Chapel Street.

Chris Moyles in the Malmaison a couple of nights before the Merseyside derby.

Soto Kyrgiakos crossing Old Hall Street near the Beetham West Tower.

Daniel Pacheco and Suso in La Vina, North John Street, on the day after January's derby.

John W Henry and Tom Werner buying sandwiches in Philpotts, Exchange Flags, a couple of days after the same game.

Ian Rush at Melwood a few days before the Wolves away game.

Status Quo drummer John Coghlan at Longmoor Primary School, Woolton and Ryan Babel at Anfield Junior School on the same day.

Dean Sullivan, Brookside's Jimmy Corkhill, in the M&S cake section.

David Hasselhoff and

Reality bites: Serial WAG Danielle Lloyd spotted in San Carlo

Amanda Holden outside The Empire, Lime Street, shortly before Wolves v LFC kicked off.

John Aldridge shopping in Sainsbury's, Woolton, the day after the 3-0 win at Wolves.

John Parrott driving through Crosby in a silver Mercedes with a blonde female in the passenger seat.

Jay Spearing in a 4x4 outside Anfield an hour before the Fulham game kicked off.

Ray Clemence, Jimmy Case and Tommy Smith hugging each other and having a laugh in the Anfield press room before Liverpool v Fulham.

Ex-Reds midfielder Michael Thomas and Bury striker Ryan Lowe in the Main Stand at the Fulham game.

Andy Carroll being driven around Woolton in a 4x4 looking at houses.

Luis Suarez taking afternoon tea in the Hope Street Hotel.

Jamie Carragher driving past the Five Lamps, Waterloo, on the Saturday before the Stoke game.

Soto Kyrgiakos complaining about the weather to a Liverpool fan who said 'hello' as walked towards Beetham's West Tower, Brook Street.

Scully star Drew Schofield in the Slaughterhouse, Fenwick Street.

Marcel Desailly tucking into a plate of food in the Stamford Bridge press-room before Liverpool's win there.

Phil Redmond stood outside the Liverpool Echo, Old Hall Street, a few days after the Chelsea game.

The Kop Mole has got spies all over the place and nothing escapes his watchful eye. From John W Henry and Tom Werner buying butties to Luis Suarez taking afternoon tea and Jamie Carragher's dad complaining about the price of flowers . . . here's a few GENUINE sightings from the past year!

Dirk Kuyt smooching with his wife in San Carlo, Castle Street.

John Aldridge chatting to a mate in the Debenhams menswear department.

Ian Callaghan in the Centenary Stand car-park after the Wigan game, walking towards Anfield Road.

Pepe Reina, wearing a ridiculous hat, on a flight to Madrid with **Michel Salgado** the day after the 1-1 draw against Wigan.

John Barnes with his wife and baby carrying Cricket shopping bags in Cavern Walks.

Philly Carragher swearing in exclamation after spotting a bouquet of flowers on sale for £100 a couple of days after Valentine's Day inside the Capital Building, Old Hall Street.

Robert Huth filling up his Porsche Panamera (which cost between £61,000-£97,000) at the Shell garage in Stoke City centre.

The Bill's Everton supporting **Andrew Lancel** at Corrie! The Musical at The Empire.

Ronnie Moran leaving Melwood with Kenny Dalglish, Steve Clarke and Sammy Lee shortly before Liverpool Reserves' friendly against Crewe at The Academy.

Johnny Vegas eating a jacket potato on a Saturday morning in Morrisons, St Helens.

Andy Carroll parking his Bentley outside the post office

in Kelsall, near Tarporley, a couple of days before the Sparta Prague home game.

A hoodie-wearing **Carlos Tevez** walking from the bus station towards Liverpool One with his arm around a mystery female the day before LFC v Sparta.

Steven Gerrard driving past Stanley Dock in his Range Rover on the same night that **Ronnie Moran** was driving through Crosby in a black Astra.

George Galloway at Warrington Bank Quay Station the day after the 1-0 win against Sparta Prague.

Adam Hammill drinking in The Village, Crosby after Wolves 4-0 win against Blackpool and in there again on the afternoon of West Ham v Liverpool.

Soto Kyrgiakos getting a lift up to the Panoramic restaurant on Brook Street.

Jamie Redknapp hanging out the back of the Sky studio.

Pepe Reina with his kids at Jungle Fun in Belle Vale shopping centre three days before LFC v Man United.

Martin Skrtel going into Café Rouge, Met Quarter with his girlfriend on the Monday after beating the Mancs 3-1.

Ricky Tomlinson nipping into the newsagents on the corner of Mersey Road and Aigburth Road on the day of the Braga away game.

Luis Suarez doing his shopping in Costco, Liverpool.

Ex-Blue nutter **Thomas Gravesen** walking down Castle Street the day before Braga v Liverpool.

So how many KOP sightings of me this time boss?

The entire Braga team walking down Old Hall Street, almost in single file, wearing grey trackies on the afternoon of their game at Anfield.

Former Liverpool, er, employee **Owen Brown** sitting outside Starbucks on Old Hall Street on the same day.

Former Bolton striker turned Stuttgart Sporting Director **Fredi Bobic** in the Main Stand at the Braga game.

Jamie Carragher telling his daughter off for walking slowly to his car after picking her up from school in Crosby.

Beth Tweddle pulling into Park Road gym, Toxteth, in a new Honda Civic with 'Beth Tweddle driven by Honda' stickers on the side.

Carly Cole pushing a pushchair through Formby Village the day before the 2-0 win at Sunderland.

Soto Kyrgiakos striding up Rigby Street wearing shades and clutching a Louis Vuitton washbag.

Jonny Evans, Kyle Lafferty and **David Healy** drinking in Yello nightclub, Belfast two days before Northern Ireland v Slovenia.

£100

One Stoke player was seen filling his Porsche... while don't be around Carra's Dad if you see expensive flowers

The view from the top as the season kicked off...

Liverpool started 2011/12 with Sunderland as the visitors to Anfield. John Henry and wife Linda were in attendance but as they took their seats, matters came to a head when Linda realised they only had 'restricted view' tickets

It was a case of one out and two in during the January transfer window. Torres showed that his armband proved nothing as he joined 'a big club' and we heralded the start of a new double act ... anyone for a bit of Luis-Carroll?

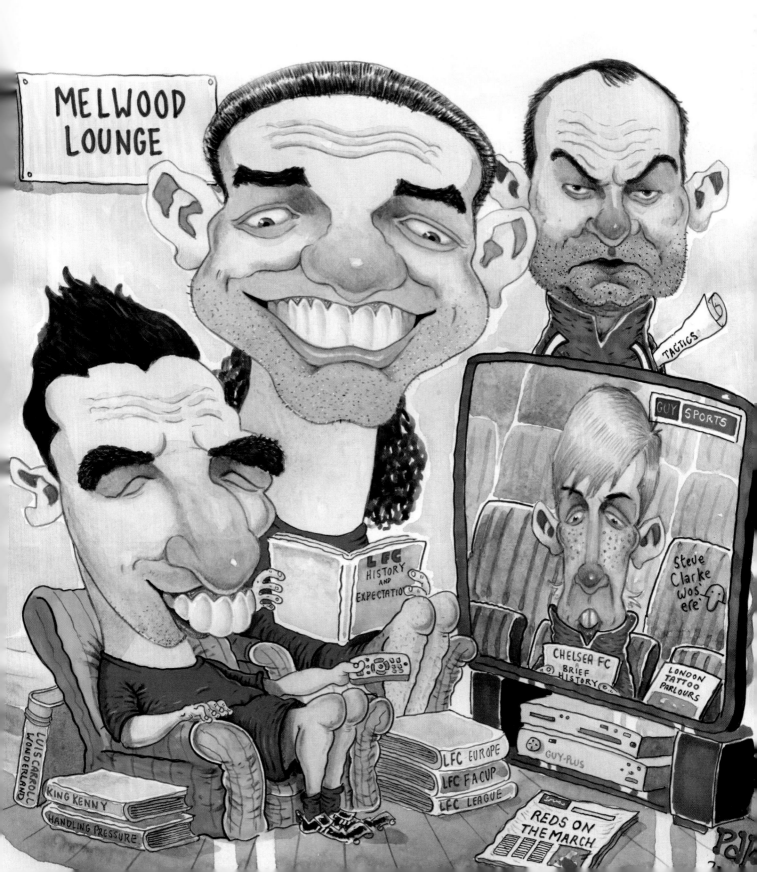

JAVIER MASCHERANO

'I know some
Liverpool supporters
were disappointed
after my exit, but this
is for them'

Blues speculate to *not* accumulate

Club	**Club | Careers | Vacancies |**
Careers	
> Equality and diversity	
> The application process	**SPECULATIVE APPLICATION - GENERAL**
> Safeguarding children	
> Vacancies	If you would like to register a general speculative application, please click on the link to the application form below.
> Speculative enquiries	
	We will retain your details on file for three months and will contact you should a suitable position arise. After three months we will contact you to see if you would like us to continue to retain your details. Should you at any time wish us to remove your
everton direct.com Everton	
> Football Kits	

LOOKS like Everton have revealed how their transfer policy operates on the club's official website.

At least we know how Victor Anichebe ended up there now...

THE KOP MOLE

With all the EXCLUSIVE news from 2011

Mancs no match on flag (or Euro) front

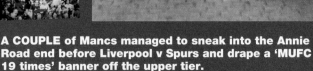

GERARD AT HIS PIQ

GERARD Pique's life could have gone one of two ways in 2008.

He could have stayed in a grim industrial English city to fight for a place in the team with Jonny Evans, won no European Cups, faced a struggle to get into the Spain squad and perhaps got together with a local celebrity like Kerry Katona.

Instead he moved to sunny Barcelona to play in a team with Xavi and Lionel Messi, won a treble-clinching European Cup for maybe the greatest club side ever, was a first-choice member of Spain's World Cup winning squad and has now got together with gorgeous Colombian hip-shaking singer Shakira, prompting Real Madrid to ban her songs from the Bernabeu.

Boy must he miss Salford.

A COUPLE of Mancs managed to sneak into the Annie Road end before Liverpool v Spurs and drape a 'MUFC 19 times' banner off the upper tier.

Turns out it was referring to how many times Man United players would touch the ball against Barcelona, but a good effort nonetheless.

Of course there was always going to be a Liverpudlian response and when it came it was rather amusing.

First of all this 'F*CK OFF FERGIE 5X' banner was unfurled outside Old Trafford, but what really tickled us was when TV cameras pictured it in the Barca end at Wembley while their fans were celebrating their 4th European Cup success.

Then, the following day, a group of Kopites unveiled this 'Barca Champions 4 times/Liverpool Champions 5' times banner outside Fergie's house in Wilmslow.

The lads then made a quick getaway in case Fergie came out. Well, he doesn't like it when things get Messi...

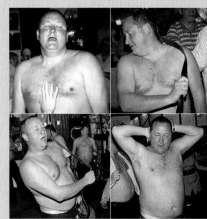

Now digging out even more Kop goss and dishing even more dirt on our rivals!

Follow us at twitter.com/thekopmagazine

Kenny's other double

■ EVER wondered where Kenny Dalglish goes for a bevvy after a game? Well, The Kop can exclusively reveal, thanks to Reds Michael Murray and Kate Buckley, that the King enjoys toasting three points with a pint down the 'Big House' in Liverpool city centre.

Well, not really... Kenny lookalike George Connor – already a Kop Mole hit in 2011 – was out celebrating following Liverpool's 2-0 victory at Arsenal in August.

You can book George for your very own Dalglish experience – although Martin Atkinson or Mike Jones may have got there first – by contacting him at *shadesofgrey051@hotmail.co.uk*.

Neville superjuice?

PHIL Neville's wife Julie has launched her own website – www.winnaturally.com – on which she sells healthy living and organic products.

She also has a blog where she writes about her juice, superfood, product and health condition of the week, which was recently 'cystitis'. "Wear cotton underwear," she advised and "avoid intercourse during an attack."

Whether Phil offers the same tactical advice on his iPhone football training app I don't know and I also can't confirm if taking the juice prevents you from scoring embarrassing derby own goals at Anfield...

THE LEAVING OF LIVERPOOL
...the transfer window deals you may have missed

IT was such a busy summer for Liverpool in the transfer market that trying to keep up with everything that went on wasn't easy. Thankfully, the Reds were able to ship out a lot of deadwood, but just in case you're not sure about who went where, here is a brief recap of the major summer departures from Anfield

David Ngog joined the Trotters...

Awight Dave

Emiliano Insua went The Lisbon

After-training special: All you can eat buffet

The Lisbon

Raul Meireles made a 'career move'

Just give me a shout and I'll help you pack... that goes for all of you

Have Volvic put a bid in yet? How about Buxton

Christian Poulsen washed up at a club naïve enough to think he's any good

And as for Degen...

Lucas had a new contract to go with his new born baby in March, although Pepe's future was still up in the air. He put his faith in Kenny though and not Mystic Meg to decide that his future was at Anfield.

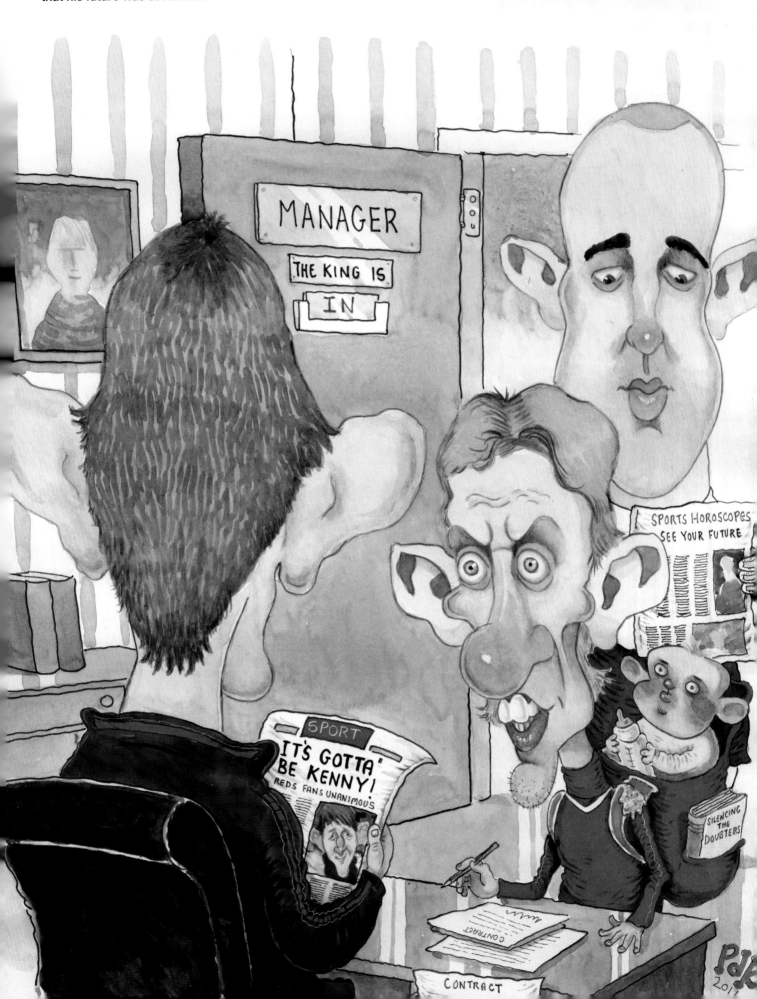

THE KOP MOLE'S PAPARAZZI PICS

When it comes to getting those highly sought after snaps, the Kop Mole is always one step ahead of the game. Over the last 12 months football's most famous gossip columnist has given Kop Magazine readers exclusive after exclusive. Here he talks us through some of his best pics of 2011

IF you're a Robbie Fowler fan and you're not on Twitter yet then you really need to sign up for an account.

The Liverpool legend – who tweets under the name @Robbie9Fowler – has one of the most entertaining Twitter pages you'll find.

Not only does he return abuse from rival fans in hilarious fashion – his response to someone claiming he was 'best buds with Mark Bosnich back in the day' was "funny you remember that because you were only young and in bed most nights when we were at yours with your mum" – but he also posts some cracking pictures such as these.

The only thing is I'm not sure which looks worse – God modelling his infamous 1996 FA Cup final suit 15 years on or the costume he wore for a Hawaiian themed fancy dress party…

STANDARD Chartered's shirt-sponsorship deal with Liverpool is worth £80 million to the Reds, but what they might not know about is the international bank's previous connections with Everton.

As my picture of Craig Johnston in a 1982 Merseyside derby shows, Standard Chartered used to have an advertising board at Goodison Park.

I'm now trying to find out if Howard Kendall secretly had a Candy washing machine…

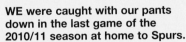 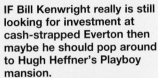

WE were caught with our pants down in the last game of the 2010/11 season at home to Spurs.

Kenny's boys had been doing brilliantly but I suppose our winning streak had to come to an end sooner or later.

At least there was an exclusive exposé during the 2-0 defeat to Tottenham in May.

Liverpool unveiled their new away kit and I was there with my camera to capture the strip in all its glory (below).

Some said it was a big flop and blamed the new 'natural' look on cost-cutting measures by the club. At least it wasn't as bad as as Everton's pink kit...

IF Bill Kenwright really is still looking for investment at cash-strapped Everton then maybe he should pop around to Hugh Heffner's Playboy mansion.

At the age of 33, former Playboy cover star Izabela Lukomska-Pyzalska (left) has taken over Polish second division strugglers Warta Poznan and pledged to run the club "with an iron fist."

Should Richard Keys be reading, an iron fist is not what women press shirts with.

I'm told that one of Lukomska-Pyzalska's rich playmates is looking to invest heavily in an English club, but only if they play in a girly pink shirt and have players with girly names.

Potentially good news for Janice Mucha, Phyllis Neville, Denise Stracqualursi, Sylvia Distin, Jackie Rodwell, Leanne Osman, Mary-Anne Fellaini, Josie Baxter, Victoria Anichebe, Rosanne Barkley and Louise Saha, then.

Anyway, enjoy this picture I took of her in her cozzy – down the local baths.

EVEN though Highbury has now been converted into apartments, the Reds still have a presence at Arsenal's old ground.

Anfield season ticket holder Simon Caplin is living in Highbury Square while working in London and makes sure that everybody knows his allegiances by hanging this flag from his window.

Thanks to Jody Roberts for the pic and I'm told that when Simon's flag flaps in the breeze it reaches the same decibel level that the North Bank used to in their heyday...

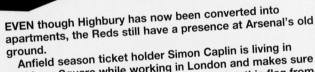

ACCORDING to one of his tweets, Everton's Seamus Coleman has been holidaying in "Villa More in Portugal."

Either he's been ripped off by a villa owner who demanded more when he found out he was a footballer, or he means 'Vilamoura' and can't spell for toffee. My money's on it being both.

Meanwhile, Tony Hibbert spent the summer break with something that best represents him as a Premier League footballer – a fish out of water.

Apparently the boyhood Red caught this 32lb 6oz whopper while fishing in Lake Chira, 5,000ft up in the mountains of Gran Canaria, and just happened to have his Everton shirt with him.

Never before has there been so much carp on one photo...

THE KOP MOLE'S PAPARAZZI PICS

I'M not entirely sure how popular it will be, but the 'Graeme Souness look' is now available in Spain.

One of my spies spotted Souey's perm and tache on a mannequin in a Madrid wig shop, although they could have belonged to Yozzer Hughes.

I'd say the look would help a big Portuguese jessie of a footballer who rubs moisturiser into his legs rather than wintergreen and spends most of his time rolling around in mock agony after the merest of touches to man up, but where would you find someone like that in Madrid?

THE Official Liverpool FC Legends 2011 desk calendar has been sat on my desk, funnily enough, since the turn of the year and displays a (fairly) slim-line Jan Molby jogging out on to the Anfield pitch.

Have a look behind Big Jan, though – is that a young Martin O'Neill leaning on the dug-out with the camera or what?

HAVING spent the season not getting the chance to dive at the dive his club play at, Everton's Reserve keeper Jan Mucha went for a dive instead.

I've absolutely no idea why, but Martin Sktrel's Slovakian international team-mate plunged into the Blue Planet Aquarium's 3.8 million-litre Caribbean Reef display at Cheshire Oaks and had his photo taken clutching a ball, presumably because it's hard to flap at one under water.

Mucha then encountered a number of sharks, including a Sand Tiger shark, which has more teeth than Everton's entire strikeforce put together.

The tank also has around 1,500 fish in it and I'm told that Mucha felt particularly at home being amongst the small fry.

(AT LEAST) two ex-Reds tied the knot and one former Blue filed for divorce in 2011, although swapping the Kop Magazine for a bride means both Mark Gonzalez and Peter Crouch are disqualified from the Kop Summer Challenge 5.

Congratulations though went to former Liverpool winger Gonzalez on his marriage to stunning Chilean dancer Maura Rivera.

The pair tied the knot in Our Lady of Carmen church in Nuñoa, Chile, on January 7 and held their wedding reception in the Parlour Ballroom of Santiago's Hyatt Hotel.

With the new Mrs Gonzalez having appeared in several TV shows in Chile, including Stars on Ice, the wedding was a huge media event and hundreds of people turned up to catch a glimpse of the couple.

Gonzalez had to wait an extra 12 months to sign for Liverpool after an independent group of 'experts' including former Chesterfield boss John Duncan and ex-Huddersfield striker Mark Lillis recommended that he shouldn't be given a work permit.

There's no word yet on whether they objected to the marriage.

SHORTLY before getting married in June, Abi Crouch offered this pearl of wisdom in Esquire: "I used to say if I got to model for Victoria's Secret I'd die happy. But now I've got a baby, I can't die because I've got to look after her."

Who'd have ever thought Peter would be the brains of the family?

A WEEK before their fourth wedding anniversary, ex-Blue Landon Donovan officially filed for divorce from his actress wife Bianca Kajlich (left), who stars in US comedy Rules of Engagement.

The LA Galaxy midfielder cited "irreconcilable differences," as the reason for the divorce.

Kajlich has yet to state why she wanted the split, but as Donovan told www.followtonians.com "I'm an Evertonian for life now," less than a fortnight after their joint announcement I've got a pretty good idea what the 'irreconcilable differences' refer to.

ANDY Carroll's appearance at Glastonbury in rather questionable clothing made the national papers, but the best performance of the festival came from a couple of Liverpool fans.

While U2 and Beyonce (amongst others) were on stage, Jo Hughes (@urbanF0xx) and Kelly Lynch (@Lynchy0were) were flying this Don't Buy The Sun banner high in the sky.

Made by Jaime Partridge, it was shown on the big screens at Glastonbury and was seen live on the BBC several times throughout their coverage of the three-day festival.

Credit to the girls and if you return to Glasto in 2013 ladies then how about a banner especially for the BBC – 'Don't Employ Kelvin MacKenzie'.

And the tweet silver song...

Like it or loathe it, the social networking site Twitter has become a great way to interact with Reds past and present. Many ex-players have signed up, including Glenn Hysen. We've had loads of entertainment following the silver-topped former Swedish defender's Twitter account – so here's some of his best twit bits from this year...

Our tweet to Glenn and his reply about one of his videos:

To @Glenn_Hysen Your video is getting a mention in The Kop Glenn - great to see YNWA still means so much to you

To @TheKopMagazine Ha ha.. I'll do anything for LFC! Great club. Great supporters and fantastic atmosphere at Anfield. Will never forget it.

The best @Glenn_Hysen tweets of 2011

3-3. Lucky Old Trafford. If United had lost Ferguson's nose would have exploded. All the best. Glenn.
- reaction to Man Utd's 3-3 draw with Basel after being 3-2 down from 2-0 up

If I marry Glen Johnson would he have been called Glen Hysén? Hysén (number 2 as well) in LFC all over again! Haha.. All the best. Glenn.
- a tweet that followed another imagining the result of actress Glenn Close marrying Saddam Hussein...

AWFUL first half! Lucas is horrible. Skrtel is too. Carroll is too. Henderson is too. Adam was. Bring on Kuyt and Bellamy! The lads need to work as a "unit", show a better body language and MAKE WAR! Dalglish usually don't scream and shout in the locker room. But I hope he did now. Use the hair blower!!! Come on Pool!
- three tweets rolled into one made at half-time of our defeat to Spurs in September. You'd think we were playing badly...

What's happening! I am having 1 shot for every Liverpool goal... They better stop now! I'm going to be wasted! Ynwa. Dalglish is the king!
- two goals in a minute against Bolton in August had Glenn

thinking he'd have an almighty hangover

Tomorrow I'll be at Bayern Munich. I'll tell them that Christian Poulsen is a FANTASTIC player and suggest a straight swap with Ribéry.. or Schweinsteiger.. Glenn.
- we're sure that's exactly the word we all would have used...

How many Evertonians does it take to change a lightbulb? None. They just sit in the dark and blame Liverpool. All the best. Glenn.
- we see watt he did there

SC Braga better watch out for a smooth Carra tonight. He's got a license to kill. YNWA. Glenn.
- Jamie Carragher's perfect tackle on Nani against the

Mancs in March invites a subtle joke from the Swede

I met this really kinky girl last night and took her home. In bed she said "humiliate me!" so I went out and bought her a Man C shirt.
- whatever floats your boat Glenn...

The best @TheKopMagazine tweets of 2011

Poulsen is going to Evian. Any chance of Peckham Spring putting in a bid for Joe Cole? 30 August

And the Oscar for best actor goes to... Rupert Murdoch #dontbuythesun 19 July

Can we be first to suggest 'Adam, Adam, Adam Adam, Adam Adam Adam, Charlie!' to the old Hamann chant #probablywontcatchon 6 July

Signing a player? In early June? Hasn't Comolli read Rick Parry's LFC manual? 9 June

Carlos Tevez thinks Manchester is boring. He should speak to Ryan Giggs. He's had a great time there. 7 June

Can see Stamford Bridge from my hotel window. Have asked to move to a room with no window. 9 May

For 119 years MUFC have never had more titles than LFC. Come back in 2130. 8 May

Strike me pink. Channel 5 have cancelled Home & Away to show LFC v Sparta tonight. Flamin' galahs. 24 February

Gary Neville has retired? Before he managed to grow his muzzie? 3 February

Ol' wobbly legs Jerzy Dudek retired from football in 2011 but after a quick glance at his website, The Kop realised that our ex-big Pole is as busy as ever. In fact, he's even launched his own reality TV series...

JERZY SHORE

A goalkeeper's 'you shall not pass' mentality serves Jerzy well as he takes up gatekeeping

A father and son scouting trip unearths sure-fire Liverpool flops Joe Cold and Momo Sissnowko

It's derby barby day at the Dudek house

Jerzy hides his frustration as the King won't tell him if he or Brucie has the best wobbly legs

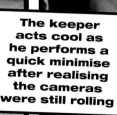

The keeper acts cool as he performs a quick minimise after realising the cameras were still rolling

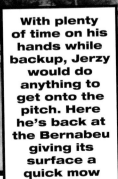

With plenty of time on his hands while backup, Jerzy would do anything to get onto the pitch. Here he's back at the Bernabeu giving its surface a quick mow

NEXT TIME: Keeping up with the Koncheskys

In the first summer with the Purs(low) strings finally loosened, Dalglish, Comolli and FSG launched their 'whatever the opposite of what Rick Parry did' transfer plan and actually had one of their top targets in the trolley in early June

Back   Forward   Stop   Refresh   Home   AutoFill   Print   Mail

LFcbaY

Anything and everything a Kopite exclusively made-up website and you've always promised yourself.

All Items   Auctions   Buy It Now

football magazine   Sporting Goods

☐ Search title **and** description

INVISIBLE MAN BANNER   Bids: **9**   Time remaining: **4 years**

A banner of pure originality, this proclamation of love for a fraud is, most importantly, a real show of class

For fans of souless clubs who not only steal from a history-steeped, legendary institution, but don't know that they're copying the Shankly Gates design when they're doing it

---

FOOTBALL MANAGER 2012   Bids: **60**   Time remaining: **3 days**

Ultra-realistic game where you can take your favourite club to the top (or reload a save without consequence if you mess up...)

Ideal training for uneducated Dalglish critics and/or clueless non-football men meddling where they are not wanted. Combine with a copy of the latest FIFA for ultimate effect

---

SKY SPORTS SUBSCRIPTION   Bids: **0**   Time remaining: **EXPIRED**

Celebrate 20 years of ~~MU~~ SKY television... *or cancel your contract and instead watch ever-improving free online streams*

Or for only £50 per month spend your Monday nights watching Ray Boy dance around a studio as he 'you know', shows you how to, 'you know', err, defend

---

POT   Bids: **1**   Time remaining: **-9 years**

A cheap yet warm-hearted gift for a neighbour in desperate need of something to p*ss in

Perfect for neighbour, counterpart or adversary – or especially all of the above – who finds himself or his employers in troubled financial difficulties

---

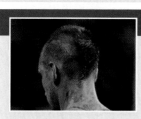

HAIR CLIPPERS   Bids: **12,500,000**   Time remaining: **12 months**

One-of-a-kind shaver used by famous Portuguese footballer now at reduced price as he no longer needs the money

Would promise better deal but have been let down in past. Unfortunately presumed either faulty or difficult to use as previous owner didn't complete last haircut...

RUBBER DUCK   Bids: **1**   Time remaining: **Until new manager**

For organisations who continually find their employees taking early baths

Managers with a track record of having player sent off more than any of the competitors on a seasonal basis can at least attempt to keep morale up

---

🌐 Internet zone

wants can be found on Lfcbay. Just log on to our
bid for that cardboard Comolli or rubber duck
Here's just a few of the items that are on sale . . .

click here)

Search Refine Search

CARDBOARD COMOLLI Bids: **38**   Time remaining: **5 years**

Get your own life-size cut-out of Liverpool's Director of Football ~~Strategy~~

Perfect for photo opportunites such as unveiling new employees or new deals for current ones. You'll think it's the real thing! A perfect picture every time

---

NON-ALCOHOLIC BEER   Bids: **1**   Time remaining: **'til Euros**

All of the taste but none of the after-effects, keep your pony-tailed striker's mind focussed on pointless friendlies

Keep putting your foot in it by needlessly criticising your national side's most expensive ever player? Why not try out this compromise for your peace of mind

---

DJ DECKS   Bids: **19**   Time remaining: **EXPIRED**

Chill out 2 da beat wiv dis well-used DJ kit (owner only worked in UK part-time – or when he felt like it)

Personalised with employee number at former job so could be ideal purchase for my replacement (SMH). Selling as too much of a nuisance to transport to Germany

---

TWITTER FOR DUMMIES   Bids: **3**   Time remaining: **UNLIMITED**

Get clued up on how to (and how not to) use the latest social network trend

The famous can take advantage by getting closer to their supporters, or by criticising referees, announcing team news early, or uploading images showing a little too much

---

SOTO'S BOOTS   Bids: **1**   Time remaining: **No comment**

Cult figure of the silent type's footwear left behind after change of employer

Worn occasionally in 2011, although may show signs of wear and tear as owner prone to rash tackles on opponents causing additional damage

---

THE BIG ONE DAY PASS   Bids: **0**   Time remaining: **1 season**

Saturday pass for Blackpool's Big One rollercoaster. Owner Mr J.Shelvey works weekends and can't use

Would suit any fan used to the stomach-churning highs and mind-numbing lows that come with following Liverpool FC over the past couple of seasons

bellamy's got the X FACTOR

KOP Karaoke is always popular at this time of the year and we've got three new classics to belt out. Oh, and if you play the songs on YouTube while reading our, er, 'updated', words, they sound even better...

THE KOP Karaoke

Someone in Blue (with apologies to Adele)

I heard that you've settled down
That you found Suarez and
you're happy now
I heard that your dreams came true
Guess he gives you things I didn't
give to you

Old friends, why are you so shy?
Ain't like you to not bounce or
tell me that I'm sh*te

I hate to turn up now dressed
in blue uninvited
But I couldn't stay away, I couldn't fight it
I had hoped you'd see my face and that
you'd be reminded
That for me it isn't over

Never mind, I'll find someone in Blue
But they're nothing like the best
like you, no
Don't forget me, I beg "just go get
f***ed," you said
Sometimes it lasts in love but
sometimes it hurts instead
Sometimes I'm crap up front but
sometimes I'm sh*t instead
Yeah

You'd know how the time flies
Only yesterday I'm the toast of your lives

I was bought then raised
In the Anfield ways
Bound by the hope of some glory days

I hate to turn up now dressed in blue uninvited
But I couldn't stay away, I couldn't fight it
I had hoped you'd see my face and
that you'd be reminded
That for me it isn't over, yeah

Never mind, I'll find someone in Blue
But they're nothing like the best like you, no
Don't forget me, I beg "ne-ver a Red," you said
Sometimes it lasts in love but
sometimes it hurts instead
Nothing compares
To Kopites down here
Regrets and mistakes
The armband was fake
Who would have known how bittersweet
this would taste?

Never mind, I'll find someone in Blue
But they're nothing like the best like you, no
Don't forget me, I beg "you're just
plastic," you said
Sometimes it lasts in love but
sometimes it hurts instead

Never mind, I'll find someone in Blue
But they're nothing like the best like you, no

Don't forget me, I beg "so who are
yer," you said
Sometimes it lasts in love but
sometimes it hurts instead
Sometimes I'm crap up front but
sometimes I'm sh*t instead

BLUE 09

BELLAMY
LFC...WITHOUT ME?

Without Me (with apologies to Eminem)

One Welsh winger goes down
the outside, down the outside,
down the outside
One Welsh winger goes down
the outside, down the outside,
down the outside

Guess who's back
Back again
Bell'my's back
Tell a friend
Guess who's back, guess who's back,
guess who's back, guess who's back,
guess who's back, guess who's back,
guess who's back...

I've come from Manchester, cause
nobody wants to see Ngog no more
They want Craigy, I'm so much better
Well if you want Craigy,
this is what I'll give ya
A little bit of golf mixed with
some hard stick yeh
Some pace-yeh that'll jump start
your heart quicker
than a shock when I get booked
on the last whistle
by the ref when I'm not co-operating
when I'm rockin' the Kop and
procrastinating (hey!)
You waited this long,
now stop the hating
Cause I'm back, I'm in the Red
and often-playing
I know that you got a job Mr Kenny
but your selection problem's
complicating
MCFC won't let me be
or let me be me, so let me see
They tried to shut me down NUFC
But it feels so quiet, without me
So, come on Ging, let's have less lip
Swing back, steady your hips,
and shout fore a bit
And get ready, cause this six
iron's fu*kin' heavy
I just settled up my contract,
f**k you City!

Now this looks like a job for me
So everybody, just follow me

Cause we need a little, controversy
Cause it feels so quiet, without me
I said this looks like a job for me
So everybody down LFC
Cause we need a little, controversy
Cause it feels so quiet, without me

A-tisket a-tasket, I go tit for tat with
anybody who's talkin this and that shit
Ke-vin Muscat, you need your
ass kicked
worse than that little pitch
invading bastard
Alan Shearer? You can't get
more squarer
You forty-one year old baldheaded bore,
go home, you don't know me, you're
too old, let go, it's over,
Nobody listens to Lawro...
Now let's go, just gimme the signal
I'll be there with a goal and list
full of insults
I been mad, vengeful with a
wedge yo ever since Riise turned
himself into a golf ball
But sometimes man it just seems
every paper only wants to discuss me
So this must mean I'm dis-gus-ting
But it's just me, not in their team
No I'm not the Welsh king
of controversy
I am the worst thing since
Bodin's penalty
to go Man City so selfishly
and use it to get myself wealthy
(Hey!) There's a concept that works
Twenty million other City players emerge
But no matter how many fish in the sea
It'll be so quiet, without me

Now this looks like a job for me
So everybody, just follow me
Cause we need a little, controversy
Cause it feels so quiet, without me
I said this looks like a job for me
So everybody down LFC
Cause we need a little, controversy
Cause it feels so quiet, without me

la-la-la-la-la, la-la-la-la-la, la-la-la-la-la,
la-la-la-la...

Imogen
(with apologies to John Lennon)

Imogen there's no headlines
It's easy if you try
No wife to hear us
Above all only lies
Imogen all the cheating
Lying every day

Imogen there's no tabloids
It isn't hard to do
Nothing to run or hide from
And no sick rumours too
Imogen all the cheating
Living lies in peace

You may say I'm a cheater
But I'm not the only one
I hope someday you'll forget us
And the claims will all be gone

Imogen no injunctions
I wonder if you can
No need for court or judges
A brother who knows nowt
Imogen all the cheating
Hushed to all the world

You may say I'm a cheater
But I'm not the only one
I hope someday you'll forget us
Cos the claims have all been wrong

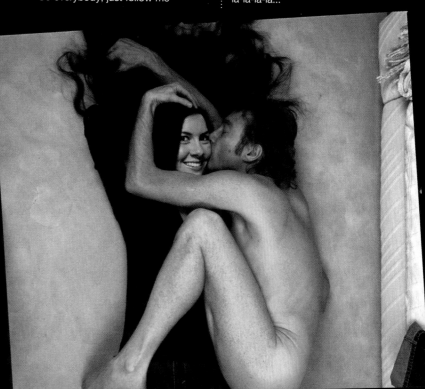

PHILIPP DEGEN'S
LIVERPOOL FOOTBALL CLUB HIGHLIGHTS:

DAVID VILLA

'I dedicate the victory to Pepe Reina's daughters, who are like my nieces'

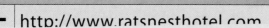
GARY Neville is spending the proceeds of his testimonial against Juventus on building a hotel and supporters club next to Old Trafford. The Kop has managed to obtain early details of the facilities that will be available in the hotel. Welcome to The Rat's Nest...

THE RAT'S NEST HOTEL
NEAR OLD TRAFFORD ★ ★ ★

| HOME | LOCATION | ROOMS & RATES | BOOKING | FACILITIES |

ALEX FERGUSON SUITE

NEIL WEBB BUFFET
(All you can eat)

GUEST ROOMS

Doubles

None available. Please visit Barcelona if you want a double.

Da Silvas (Twin rooms)

- Two single beds (can be pushed together if staying with family member)
- En-suite bathroom with 'Vidic' (early) shower
- Wi-fi (not to be confused with wife-eye, Ryan, you'll be fine)
- Black out curtains (ideal for hiding the horrendous view)
- 32-Inch LCD TV (BBC not available in the Alex Ferguson suite)
- Pay-Per View TV (please note if you watch MUTV this will show up as 'room service' on your bill to avoid embarrassment)
- Safe (to keep Scousers from robbing your stuff)
- Mini Bar (filled with whisky in the Alex Ferguson suite)
- Hairdryer treatment
- 'Pot calling the kettle black' tea-making facilities (ideal for those who sing Wayne Rooney's name and You Scouse b@st@rds)
- Complimentary toiletries (does not include razor)
- 24-hour Room Service (unless Michael Carrick is on then you'll get no service at all)

ARRIVAL AND DEPARTURE

Check-in: **2pm**
Czech-out: **Karel Poborsky**

DIRECTIONS

On arrival at Heathrow (Terminal 4) take the M40, M42, M6, A556 and A56 to Old Trafford. The Rat's Nest is on Sir Matt Busby Way and is full of vermin. Parking is available underground, in the Sewer Car Park.

PET POLICY

- **Rats allowed**
- **Dogs not allowed (unless they're with you, Wayne)**

DINING   **FIND US**   **SPECIAL OFFERS**   **CONTACT US**

NO BEAUTY TREATMENT
(ugly treatment available)

LEISURE FACILITIES

- Swimming pool (with Kop Magazine buried underneath)
- Fully equipped gym (please note the cross-trainer is not Mike Phelan in a bad mood)
- No beauty treatment (ugly treatment available)
- Pedicures (pay for five toes on one foot and get your 6th done free)
- ManUcures (make your nails look nice for when holding three fingers up)

CONFERENCE FACILITIES

- Room available for press briefings (please note we may threaten to 'get you' if you ask a perfectly reasonable question we don't like)

CONFERENCE FACILITIES

DINING AND DRINKS

- Neil Webb buffet (all you can eat)
- Catalan Cuisine (a taste of Europe's finest)
- Paul McGrath Bar (open 24 hours)

LFC CHRISTMAS FANCY
DRESS PARTY, 1990.
BRUCIE, BIG JAN & STAN

KOP CLASSIFIEDS

Golf Lessons

NEED to improve your swing? Stutter with the putter? Want to get a hole in ~~John~~ One? Give Craig a bell on 0151 444 444.

███████ Services

CAUGHT by the press with your kecks down? Get a Super-Injunction with ███████ lawyers. Our clients include ███████! and of course ███████. Call 01███████69 now and give us the gig.

France

NEED to get away? Feel knackered after 15 minutes on a pitch? Escape to Lil' Joe's B&B, France. English owner, you won't even notice I'm here. No booking charge, £100k per week. Lone visitors welcome.

Sale now on

REDUCED!
Genuine Ngog socks
Now only £4!

MISSING

ITALIAN show pony. Expensive. Long hair and strange eyes. Answers to the name Alberto. Missing since August. Also went missing last August. Last seen at John Lennon Airport. Any info call 0151 178 178.

58 Today
YAKUBU

To our beautiful baby Yak. Here's to many more years of ~~toffees~~ fried chicken. Love & best wishes, BRFC x

HEALTH

DR. DALGLISH

I prescribe tried and tested attacking pass-and-move football

Going insane thanks to a leader you don't believe in? Suffering from stress?

Call on Dr. Dalglish and you'll soon feel 20 years younger.

Health tip:
Clap nine times to the following rhythm -
clap, clap
clap clap clap
clap clap clap clap -
and then shout 'DALGLISH!'
and the feelgood factor will be instantly restored*.

* Uneducated FIFA12 know-it-alls note: Does not guarantee a 100% win ratio

Personal

SWISS male, 28, BSOP, unattached, seeks football club with good physio for treatment and maybe more.
Call Philipp, Box no 27.

Clothing

NOW in stock, South American coats, made in Uruguay, perfect for the taller gentleman. Also still on offer from our latest ladies range: Maxi dresses & Skrts. Please note: Christian LouPoulsen shoes are no longer available

Wanted

DEFENDERS must have no pace or skill. Positional sense not necessary. Call Arsene before January.

Deaths

TORRES - Fernando September 18, 2011. Died of embarrassment. Went clean through at Old Trafford and sadly missed.

Craig's Cross-words

Do you know as many cross-words as Craig?

ACROSS
1. Alan Shearer (6)
2. To strike a Norwegian with a six-iron (4)
DOWN
1. Message to opponent, _ _ _ _ off (4)
2. Fatherless matchday official (7)
3. You can kiss this if you don't like me (4)

Solution: ACROSS 1. w*nker 2. tw*t DOWN 1. f*ck 2. b*stard 3. arse

Used Footballers

webuyanystar.com

WE buy any star.com,
Any name, any age, any price, any player,
We buy any star.com,
Just enter your cash figure now at
We buy any star.com,
Injured, past it, how ever many million,
Just enter your cash figure now at
We buy any star.com.

Tickets

REDS in Europe 2011/12

Liverpool Football Club have received an allocation of 0 tickets for these NON-ticket, non-fixtures priced as follows:

Adult £45
Over 65s £35
Children £35

Sale details:
August 1, 2011: Season ticket holders, Members and Fan Card holders who attended Ferencvaros (1967), Dresden (1978), Dundalk (1982) **and** Mypa 47 (1996)

Supporters can purchase NO tickets per qualifying Fan Card and a maximum of NONE per transaction. Please note there will be a £2.50 per ticket booking fee for reading this advert.

We would emphasise to all eligible applicants that no tickets are available and no guarantees can be given that they will be next season either.

We celebrated the return of the one and only King in January with this cartoon. Sammy Lee was jester in time to feature before heading out of Anfield later in the year

EVERTON FC

★ ★ ★ ★

The search for investment continues...

Everton haven't won a pot for 16 years and now they can't even afford to buy one to p*ss in. Evertonians are revolting, and they're not too happy with how the club is being run either, so Bill Kenwright and David Moyes have upped their search for new investment...

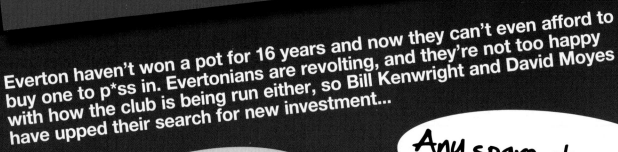

Spare the price of a new stadium?

Any spare change?

New York * Paris * Walton

Job Lot

KEYS & GRAY: Jobs for the boys

Richard Keys and Andy Gray won't recall the Wolves v Liverpool game from January very fondly, but at least they have gone on to find work after their controversial exit from Sky. We can reveal what they tried their (hairy) hands at before landing a job on the radio...

Can you explain the offside rule to me again?

Andy seemed well suited as judge of the Miss World contest

You beauty... you beauty... you beauty

Woah Sami Sami - Finn picks up pace

HE used to drive a mini when he was at Liverpool but Sami Hyypia has swapped it for something a little racier since he retired.

The Giant Finn was Sheikh Khalid Al Qassimi's co-driver as the Abu Dhabi World Rally driver warmed up in his Ford Fiesta for Finland's Neste Oil Rally.

"That was one of the most thrilling moments of my life," said Sami after getting out of the car. What, even more thrilling than playing alongside Igor Biscan at centre-half?

The World Rally Championship is held over 13 stages and I'm told the toughest race is in Turkey where drivers have to negotiate the roads of Istanbul to get to the Ataturk Stadium.

THE KOP MOLE

With all the EXCLUSIVE news from 2011

Rafa busy making signings

WHENEVER Rafa Benitez comes into Liverpool for the afternoon he gets mobbed and there was one crazy scene in particular when he was spotted walking up Old Hall Street with former member of his back-room staff Owen Brown.

Having posed for several pictures outside The Exchange, Rafa made it as far as Sainsbury's before a queue of people after autographs formed in front of him.

Amongst them, clutching anything they could get him to sign, were Sainsbury's staff who had rushed out of the shop – which didn't impress one customer who was left stood at the cash-tills shouting "any chance of getting served here?"

She must've been a blue.

Alright La-crosse

AS unlikely as it seems, an American company founded by the bloke who invented the titanium lacrosse stick will be manufacturing Liverpool's kits from 2012/13.

The Reds reportedly signed an English record £25-million-a-season deal with Warrior Sports, dwarfing their last £12-million-a-season contract with adidas.

Warrior Sports have been a subsidiary of New Balance (who are Boston Red Sox official footwear and apparel sponsor) since 2004, but they were formed by former Lacrosse star David Morrow in 1992 after he broke 25 aluminium sticks in a single season and came up with the idea to make them from titanium.

Morrow is still in charge at Warrior Sports and it's believed his first project will be to solve a similar breakage problem Liverpool started with in 2011/12 by making a back-four out of titanium.

Shirty Toffees come unstuck after another LFC blue-per

THE best thing about Everton having a sly dig at Liverpool is that they always end up looking more foolish themselves.

Take naming the club shop in Liverpool One as Everton Two, for instance, only for them to fail to notice that their Everton One club shop is in Liverpool 4.

If that wasn't funny enough, they thought they were having a cheap laugh at our expense when they started selling this 'local/Norwegian' t-shirt on www.evertonfc.tv – which sold out – but forgot to take into account this 'Everton Fan Map' on their official website where Blues supporters mark where they come from.

Stretches quite close to Oslo that County Road, eh?

Now digging out even more Kop goss and dishing even more dirt on our rivals!

Follow us at twitter.com/thekopmagazine

Pepe's Fun Day

HAD he not already committed his future to Liverpool then the above picture might just have started a tabloid rumour.

Two days before the Champions League final one of my spies took this snap of Pepe Reina wearing over-sized headphones on an easyJet flight from Liverpool to Barcelona.

But rather than return to Spain for secret talks with Barca, Pepe had plenty of other things lined up, namely promoting the Gillette Fusion Proglide razor, making appearances on TV shows 'Punta Pelota' and 'El Hormiguero,' commentating on the Champions League final for TVE and attending the birth of his son Luca in Cordoba.

There was one startling revelation to come from one of his TV appearances, though, when he was asked: "Have you ever spat on the ball before passing it to the rival's team?" "Well," responded Pepe, "I have to admit it. Yes."

Please let it have been against Everton, Man United or Chelsea!

THE WHYAYEPAD

Introducing the tablet computers, pet, designed especially for the Geordie people because we're different – Ye knaa what ah mean leik?

16:02   44%

Haway Pet
find somewhere to take your pet haway on holiday

Gazza Rescue
in trouble? Use this App and Gazza will come to your rescue

Forehead Frenzzy
can you make it right the way across Ant's head before your time runs out?

Dec Chairs
can you help little Dec climb onto the chair before he shouts 'get me out of here?'

Newkie Town
find the places that stock your favourite 10-bottle tipple on a Saturday night

Byker Grove
Hell's Angel? We'll help you find a property on THE street in Newcastle to live on

Chezz'll Dress Yer!
Cheryl tells you if you're wearing too many clothes to be a true Geordie lass on a neet out

wye-ayeTunes
all your favourites from Jimmy Nail and Robson Green

Shirts Direct
overweight? We'll help you find a Newcastle shirt that still fits

Angry Birds
can you make a Geordie girl wear a coat?

Shzzzzzearer
slip off to sleep to the dulcet tones of Alan Shearer talking tactics

Weather
find out whether there's fog on the Tyne

Geordie Translate
translates English so ye can understand it leik

geordiejungle

emails from me mam

all me pics man

wye-ayePod

Whose ground is it anyway?

AS you may have noticed, we tend to extract the urine somewhat in the Kop Annual, but as a famous man never said all play and no work makes Jill a dull girl. Therefore, we thought we'd launch a new game this year – Where Are We? All of the grounds are pictured from Google Street View and we've given you an extra clue by revealing when Liverpool last played there. All you need to do is work out - Where Are We?

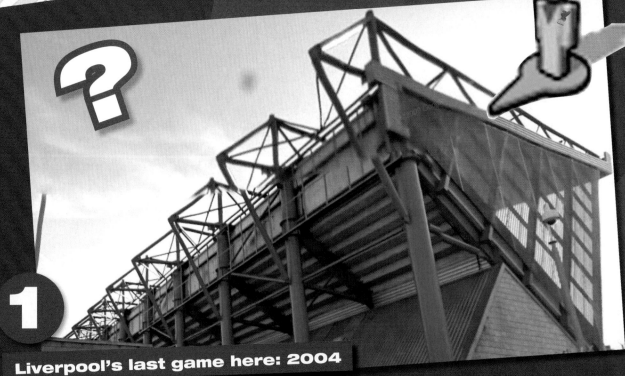

1

Liverpool's last game here: 2004

2

Liverpool's last game here: 1958

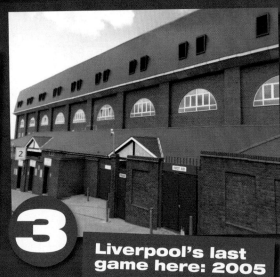

3

Liverpool's last game here: 2005

4

Liverpool's last game here: 2009

5

Liverpool's last game here: 1984

?

6

Liverpool's last game here: 1963

7

Liverpool's last game here: 1999

8

Liverpool's last game here: 2001

9

Liverpool's last game here: 2002

Whose ground is it anyway?

10

Liverpool's last game here: 1991

11

Liverpool's last game here: 1994

?

12

Liverpool's last game here: 1999

Dirk Kuyt just couldn't get enough of Luis Suarez (and Nani's) service as he scored his first Reds hat-trick past his Big Friendly Giant buddy Edwin van der Sar in March, while everyone else couldn't get enough of Fergie's media blackout where he was as quiet as the away end was that day...

You Ask, We Answer

THE wife came home from work a couple of nights ago and asked if I would pay for her to have a vajazzle for Christmas.

Not knowing what this was, I googled it and discovered that a vajazzle is a tw*t covered in blinging jewellery.

I've subsequently put in a bid for El-Hadji Diouf.

*Appy Arry,
Chigwell*

A: A generous gift, but something she'll soon get tired of.

HAVING read the Kop Annual every year since it started I am absolutely flabbergasted with the number of jokes about my weight.

One minute you call me Fat Frank, the next you say I'm overweight.

When I saw you use the word 'obese' I was in two minds whether or not to sue you, but I'm bigger than that.

Slim Frank Lampard, London

A: You said it...

I BUMPED into a Jari Litmanen lookalike in our local newsagents. He was buying 20 Benson & Hedges and a packet of extra strong mints. Do I win a prize?

*Brian Straw-Clutcher,
Hants*

A: Is this some sort of bad joke? Again.

HAVING been happily married for a number of years things started to get a little stale so following the example set by Ryan Giggs I thought I'd start an affair with my brother's missus.

Unfortunately a journalist found out about this and I've had to spend thousands on getting a super-injunction to stop them printing revelations that my brother doesn't have a missus.

Phil Anderer, Manchester

A: A classic case of being caught with your pants up.

MY kids are sceptical about global warming, they say it may even be a conspiracy by scientists to make money, but I am convinced that our winters are now a lot milder than they used to be.

I can even recall it being

so cold in Newcastle during one 1990s winter that an igloo formed around Kevin Keegan while he was conducting a training session while Terry McDermott was forced to wear his wife's boots because of slippery conditions under foot.

My kids reckon I'm making it up. Am I?

N. Vironment, Warwickshire

A: Clearly not. Show this photo to your kids the next time you turn the heating down a notch.

FOR the last five years a Bluenose work colleague has been repeatedly telling me that there's nobody better than Mikel Arteta.

Imagine my surprise, then, when having seen the best little Spaniard he knows sold to Arsenal he claimed that Arteta had been crap for the last two seasons and Everton are better off without him.

I've also noticed that he no longer talks about feeding the Yak, leading me to wonder if the RSPCA should be informed?

Stanley Dock, Bootle

A: The RSPCA should be informed about all Evertonians, but you shouldn't worry about the Yak going hungry.

I HAVE it on good authority, from a lad who knows a bloke who drinks with his cousin's former room-mate in the Flat Iron, that Liverpool's failure to qualify for Europe this season was an 'inside job'.

My contact says a rival with a personal vendetta against Liverpool FC managed to infiltrate the club by getting one of his cronies a high-profile job but no-one at Anfield realised what was going on until it was too late.

No names were mentioned when I was told this, can you shed any light on the matter?

Col Lusion, Speke

A: I believe the photo below may tell you everything you need to know.

AS a dyslexia sufferer I find it difficult to write letters, but I need to make my thoughts on this public. Mark Lawrenson is a shathouse and a twit. Thanks.

*Wojciech Tyscklvnyiv,
Palond*

A: I could've put it better myself.

CAN you put my mind at rest, please? Is Pat Nevin a real person or did a garden gnome on Channel 5

start talking tactics at me after I'd had a heavy night on the meow meow?

Doris Green, Croxteth

A: Please stop putting your mental health at risk. Watch another channel.

WHEN Liverpool put in a scoreboard at Anfield people complained about it breaking with tradition, but I now believe it to have been a good thing.

It has certainly saved me the effort of singing 'Binman, what's the score' during the Anfield Merseyside derby as all I need to do now is look to my right to ascertain such vital information.

If Liverpool hadn't installed the scoreboard, with Southall having retired, I would've had to wait until my bins were emptied on a Tuesday morning to see how LFC were getting on, which wouldn't be acceptable in this day and age.

Torben Thickmick, Kirkby

A: Well played LFC! You would have been down in the dumps all weekend!

I WISH to call into question another one of Bill Shankly's famous quotes.

He once said: "At a football club, there's a holy trinity - the players, the manager and the supporters. Directors don't come into it. They are only there to sign the cheques."

I've always taken the great man's word as gospel but are we really expected to believe that John W Henry wrote a cheque for £35 million for Andy Carroll when it would have been quicker to use his debit card or PayPal?

I'm beginning to think Shanks' views have become outdated.

*Eimar Bitslow,
Litherland*

A: It appears that Shankly's underlying message may have been lost on you.

HELLO. My dog is a massive red and shares a first name with Charlie Adam so I've written a blog about it. Any chance of a re-tweet?

*Johnny Nofollowers,
Coventry*

A: No. Please RT.

I RECENTLY received an email from LFC advertising a credit card with 0% interest. If nobody else is interested why do they think that I would be?

Ash Strapped, Runcorn

A: Credit where it's due - a good point well made.

IS it true that Luis Suarez is so difficult for opponents to stop that the Premier League have granted permission for him to be tied up on the touchline before kick-off and he is only allowed to enter the pitch after untangling himself?

Kenny Understandit, Glasgow

A: As my photo proves, this unfair PL regulation has been approved.

NOW that Manchester City are so rich because of their Arab owners, I've decided to hit back at them by boycotting oil.

I now ride a push-bike, grill my chips and refuse to recognise that Popeye has a girlfriend.

I'd like to urge all your readers to follow my example to prevent City from having a financial advantage over the rest of us.

D Luded, Wakefield

A: I just hope you've not got a baby with dry skin.

AFTER seeing Liverpool clear out all the deadwood during the transfer window, my Everton supporting mate sent a letter to David Moyes urging him to do the same.

I'm no expert, but does he really think the Everton manager has the time to dismantle the Bullens Road stand?

Seamus Kopite, Dublin

A: It's not like he's going to be busy in the transfer market...

AFTER a shopping trip into town one Saturday afternoon I got on to the bus home only to

discover it was full of Liverpool fans who were being rowdy and singing what sounded like a Depeche Mode song. Do these 'fans' get off on ruining people's journeys?

Kerry Angry, Newsham Park

A: No. They get off at the stop before The Albert.

CAN you confirm that Jamie Carragher once carried on playing in a match for Liverpool despite being struck by a bottle of Omega 3 tablets?

Sam Mon, Fishguard

A: Yes. He only suffered super fish oil injuries.

I'VE heard a rumour that when John W Henry bought Liverpool, Bill Kenwright tried to take advantage of his lack of local knowledge by telling him all LFC fans wanted a shared stadium.

Apparently he even showed Mr Henry where to build it?

Bill Dyerown, Anfield

A: Funnily enough...

* Brought to you in association with season tickets containing a serial number, not seat number, that ends in a 6, 7, 8 or 9. Spare voucher number 24 is required.

* MANAGERS - ensure you keep earning during a period of unemployment by launching a personal website that contains tactical insight which could have prevented you from becoming unemployed in the first place had you followed your own advice.
Rafael, Wirral

* WAYNE Rooney – please return from Libya at once. The large bounty on Colonel Gadaffi's head isn't what you think it is.
Slur Alex, Salford

* RECREATE the atmosphere of a Merseyside derby every day by wearing Liverpool's new 3rd strip while you look into a mirror and shout 'blue and white shite, hello, hello' repeatedly for a minute.
Lee ver Pool, Anfield

* MANCHESTER United fans – make yourselves look stupid by paying over-the-odds to service an American businessman's debts so you can sit in a football ground and sing 'we do what we want'.
I Ronnielost, Basildon

* EXPERIENCE what it's like to play in a World Cup game for England by filling your bath with treacle and trying to run in it while simultaneously watching a German sprint contest on TV.
Gareth Barry, Manchester

* MAKE it feel like it's transfer deadline day every day by standing at the bottom of Harry Redknapp's drive with a video camera and simply waiting until he pulls over in his car to tell you about all the triffic players he isn't signing.
Ryan Cygnetson, Iselworth

* IF you receive an email entitled 'two free tickets for Everton game' do not open it. It contains two free tickets for an Everton game.
Gudad Vice, Oslo

* MERSEYSIDE Police – park a big yellow police van in the middle of the junction for Walton Breck Road and Oakfield Road at full-time of every Liverpool match to cause an unnecessary bottle-neck of fans trying to get away from Anfield.
Warren Arlarse, Whiston

* PUNISH fans of clubs only good enough to be in the Football League by making them stay up past midnight to see Steve Claridge say a few critical words about their defending from set-pieces.
B.B. Seeone, London

* WHEN spending £50 million on a product that turns out to be well past its' best-before date, always keep the receipt.
R Abramovich, West London

* STRENGTHEN your marriage and get a holiday in the sun by cheating on your wife with the ex-girlfriend of a team-mate, your brother's missus or prostitutes.
Can't Say, Nottellingher

* EARN over-the-top media praise in your retirement by lunging at opponents with your studs up for 15 years safe in the knowledge that it'll be put down to you not being able to time tackles instead of thuggery.
Scholsey, Oldham

* SAVE on the use of cutlery and get your tea thrown into your face every night by saying to your girl-friend 'do us a favour, love' before handing her a pile of ironing.
Dickie Keys, ex-Iselworth

* RELIVE the London riots every night by purchasing the official history of Millwall FC DVD and playing it on the 46-inch telly you lifted from Curry's.
Pwopah Nawty, Bermondsey

* STAY on your feet.
Ray Wilkins, London

* PRETEND to be a Premier League striker by wearing an Everton shirt with 'Anichebe' on the back and scoring a goal every four years.
Big Boi, Lagos

The Torres chelsea gallery

The city was on fire, but he wasn't

When he played Liverpool he was the invisible man and the Reds won

At least his mate Raul joined him at the Bridge

Owner sees miss of season

He'll soon be bringing out a new book called 'I Love Chelsea'

Torres wasn't keen when Roman suggested a game of Russian roulette

Kung fu kick.
A new aggressive
side to his game

I am an ankle

I am an arse

I am an ear

I am an elbow

Body language
is all wrong

Big dummy.
Tantrums when
he didn't get the
right pass

In Kenny Dalglish's first spell as manager he signed club legend John Barnes as his left winger. Stewart Downing will hope to be his modern day Digger, with the King doing everything he can to help him perform anything like the legend did back in the late 80s...

The best of SPOTTED

Didi Hamann getting his hair done in Universal Studios, Dale Street.

Pepe Reina buying deodorant in Boots, Speke Retail Park.

Andy Carroll shopping in Asda, Smithdown Road.

England Under-16 manager Kenny Swain arriving at Melwood for a meeting.

Channel 4 Racing's Derek Thompson at Melwood the day after LFC v City.

Jamie Carragher high-rolling down Coronation Road, exchanging pleasantries with a long-haired passer-by.

Martin Skrtel licking a blue ice lolly while strolling through Calderstones Park with his girlfriend and pugs a few days after April's Arsenal game.

Jamie Carragher with dad Philly in a '23 Foundation' van in West Derby.

Jennifer Ellison driving a white 4x4 down Islington on Maundy Thursday.

Mark Wright, looking like he'd lost someone, in the White Star, Mathew Street on the same night.

Luis Suarez driving his family through Childwall Fiveways an hour after the 5-0 win against Birmingham.

Damien Comolli and family chilling out in Costa Coffee, Met Quarter, on the afternoon of the Royal Wedding.

Nigel Spackman tucking into a pie while stood outside Fulham's press-room toilet before Liverpool's 5-2 win at Craven Cottage.

Luis Suarez and his wife pushing a trolley around Tesco, Allerton a couple of days after.

Ian Rush carrying Louis Vuitton hand-luggage as he got off a Virgin train at Lime Street a couple of days before May's Spurs game.

Roy Evans heading into the Matou pan Asian restaurant at the Pier Head.

Tommy Smith doing his shopping with the wife in Tesco, Litherland.

Vanessa Feltz walking towards a patisserie in Soho, London.

Peter Crouch and Abi Clancy in Basement 20, Hardman Street, after Liverpool v Spurs.

Boxing promoter Frank Maloney standing outside Sakura, Exchange Flags, chatting on his phone.

Daniel Agger in Pret A Manger, Liverpool One, on the day his charity auction for soldiers injured in Afghanistan was announced.

Brian Reade drinking Birra Moretti in The Belvedere Arms, Falkner Street a few days before Villa away.

Stig Inge Bjornebye outside the Hard Day's Night Hotel on the midweek after the Villa match.

Gordon Strachan queuing to get into Universal Resort, Florida, a couple of days after Barcelona 3 Manchester United 1.

Andy Carroll and his girlfriend buying bananas in Sainsbury's, Crosby.

Former Everton defender John Bailey wandering around aimlessly outside Debenhams.

Steven Gerrard chatting to Liverpool fans in the departure lounge at John Lennon International Airport.

Beth Tweddle walking past John Lewis, Liverpool One, clutching what looked like a pasty.

Djibril and Jude Cisse visiting Claire House, Bebington.

Pako Ayestaran reading The Metro on the 8.24am Hoylake to Liverpool service on June 7.

Jay Spearing driving down Moor Lane, Crosby, in a silver Mercedes.

Charlie Adam at the services on the M6 toll road.

Phil Thompson walking down Mathew Street in a pair of shades.

David Price looking at the new 3rd strip on the day it was launched in the club shop at Liverpool One.

Gavin Winstanley (the Liverpool-supporting Scouser who got sacked on The Apprentice) in Costa Coffee, Allerton Road.

Charlie Adam opening Salon 30 hairdressers in Freckleton, Preston.

Steven Gerrard having a meal in the Blue Mallard, Burscough.

Kirstie Alley walking down Madison Avenue, New York, on June 26.

Ex-member of Rafa Benitez's backroom staff Owen Brown having his lunch in Franklins Deli, St Paul's Square.

Pako Ayestaran drinking in Pogue Mahones, Seel Street, on July 7.

Catchphrase legend and secret Liverpool fan Roy Walker shopping in M&S, Belfast.

Charlie Adam having a meal with his fiance Sophie in Sakura, Exchange Flags, the day after signing for Liverpool.

Roy Keane walking down a street in Hale, near Manchester, saying "alright lads" to a group of passing blokes who were shocked to see him.

The Kop Mole has got spies all over the place and nothing escapes his watchful eye. From present and former Reds enjoying ice creams to Andy Carroll buying bananas, and (thankfully) ex-Red Philipp Degen letting the side down off the pitch after all his damage on it . . . here's a few GENUINE sightings from the past year!

Jimmy Nesbitt dragging three bags of luggage through London Euston station.

Steven and **Alex Gerrard** with their kids on the train from London Euston to Liverpool on the day the LFC squad flew to China for the Asia tour.

Sammy Lee having a meal in San Carlo with a group of around 12 people the night before Guangdong v LFC.

Gloucester Rugby's **Mike Tindall** playing golf at Formby Hall before attending Lynsey Dalglish's wedding with Zara Phillips.

The Scaffold's Liverpool supporting **John Gorman** singing 'God save our gracious team' at the Wirral Festival of Firsts, Hoylake.

Mark Wahlberg driving past Venice Beach, California, in a massive SUV.

Liverpool doctor **Zaf Iqbal** driving through West Derby in a BMW with 'ZAF' on the licence plate.

Cindy Lauper drinking in El Tomas, La Latina, Madrid the night after Liverpool's friendly defeat at Hull.

Ronnie Whelan putting coins into a parking machine outside the Albany apartments on Old Hall Street on the day of the Galatasaray game.

UK Open champion **Darren Clarke** wearing pink shorts as he bought pizza and chips in Coast Pizza, Portrush.

Marouane Fellaini walking past HMV, Liverpool One, on the morning of Everton's friendly at Birmingham.

Michael Starke (Sinbad from Brookside) walking through Chavasse Park on the same day.

Steve Arnold (Ashley Peacock from Corrie) using the Barclays cash-point in Stockton Heath.

Warrington Wolves centre **Matt King** having a meal in The Hollow Tree, Stretton.

Bruce Jones (Les Battersby from Corrie) talking on his mobile phone in the doorway of The Mailcoach pub, Conway.

Former Olympic high-jumper **Steve Smith** watching Everton v Villarreal in the Freshfield Hotel, Formby.

Rafa Benitez signing autographs on the balcony of a Centenary Stand executive box before LFC v Valencia.

Blackpool striker **Gary Taylor-Fletcher** in the Main Stand for the 2-0 win against Valencia.

Ian Ayre and goalkeeping coach **John Achterberg** in Alma de Cuba, although not together, after the 1-1 draw with Sunderland.

Rehab fitness coach **Jordan Milsom** queueing up for Garlands on a Saturday night.

Steven Gerrard at a family do at Whiston Social Club, Paradise Lane, the day after the Sunderland match.

Jimmy Case having a pint sat outside The Other Place, Allerton Road, on the same afternoon.

Tranmere's ex-Reds right-back **David Raven** having a Magnum ice-cream near to the Hilton Hotel, Liverpool One.

Ian St John and **Ron Yeats** signing photos in the Capital Building, Old Hall Street.

Ian Callaghan walking down Anfield Road towards The Arkles after Liverpool's 3-1 win against Bolton.

Jamie Carragher wearing a suit as he dined with a friend in San Carlo, Castle Street after the Bolton game.

Dirk Kuyt wearing a suit as he dined with two friends in San Carlo, Castle Street after the Bolton game.

Danny Wilson in smart attire as he dined with several friends in San Carlo, Castle Street after the Bolton game.

Phillip Degen wearing tatty jeans and a cap as he dined with **Stephen Sama** in San Carlo, Castle Street after the Bolton game.

Wolves winger **Adam Hammill** watching Arsenal's 8-2 defeat to Manchester United in The Village pub, Crosby.

John Aldridge driving down Queen's Drive near to Childwall Fiveways a couple of days later.

Jack Robinson walking down Whitechapel with a female friend during the international break.

Adrian Chiles in the post office on Chiswick High Road, Chiswick, London.

Abi Clancy seen at Basement 20 with Crouchy

ZAF

THE **KOP**

DERBY LEGEND

MARTIN ATKINSON

Kenny Dalglish got the Reds in shape on their
return to Melwood for pre-season training as the
good old values and philosophies finally returned

THE past year has been another great one for Kop Summer Challenge 5 entries. As usual, you've been to all four corners of the world with The Kop magazine, getting your photos taken at as obscure and far-flung places as ever before. There are many great shots from a famous face to a famous (but fictional) local. Another Kopite knocked one out of the park by being the first to take the challenge at our owner's other sporting venture in Boston. Can anyone top this lot for next year? It's over to you...

The best of
Summer CHALLENGE

The Kop Magazine, Liverpool

IT seems inconceivable that a programme featuring a load of farmers from an obscure Yorkshire village would attract any TV viewers, but Sky still show Leeds United matches anyway.

Following protests against the way he is running the club, Ken Bates described Leeds fans as 'morons' which provoked a furious response from morons all over the country.

Life is far more peaceful over in Emmerdale – there hasn't been a plane crash, barn fire or apocalyptic storm there for ages – so life-long Dundee-based Red Andy Stewart decided it was safe enough to visit the village during a summer tour of England.

He gave a five-fingered salute outside The Woolpack, the second most famous boozer in the whole of Yorkshire. The first was Brian Clough, for 44 days.

Harry Kewell's wife Sheree appeared in Emmerdale as Tricia Dingle until 2004 when she was killed off after being hit by a falling tree, which was hugely ironic as her husband spent half of his career on the tree-tment table getting splinters in his arse – an injury that ruled him out for a year.

Amongst the other places Andy visited was Blackpool where he ended up having a pint with Charlie Adam, who went to school with his mate. "Charlie is a great person," Andy told us, "I hope he's a success with LFC." He will be.

SCOUSER Simon Jeffery has been doing voluntary work in Zimbabwe and as you can see from this photo he is still able to afford to travel by taxi occasionally.

They say an elephant never forgets which makes them incredibly useful taxis as you shouldn't have to tell them where to go when it's time to take you home.

Simon visited the Imire Safari Lodge, not to be confused with the Imre Varadi Lob, near Harare on his day off and took the Kop Summer Challenge 5 on the back of Ronaldinho.

The bloke controlling the elephant claimed to be a Manchester United supporter but took the Summer Challenge 5 anyway after Simon took him to tusk and let him read The Kop.

Coventry City are the only English football league club to feature an elephant on their badge, which is kind of fitting as the Ricoh Arena is a white elephant.

The stadium is one of six venues that will host the football at the London Olympics next year but was only selected after Aston Villa withdrew Villa Park because "the club has confirmed that it is considering plans for major development work." Alex McLeish was then brought in to start demolishing their squad.

ACONCAGUA is the highest mountain in the Americas, standing at 22,841 feet.

You won't find anything standing so tall in Liverpool, mainly because a steward would ask it to sit down so kids can see at the back.

Located in the Argentine province of Mendoza, the mountain is part of the Andes, as is Andes Carroll. The Liverpool striker has been described as a man-mountain, which is rather odd as when was the last time Ben Nevis or Everest grew a pony-tail?

Carroll is brilliant in the air but at £35 million he's the most expensive thing seen in our skies since Ryanair put their excess baggage charges up. We now owe Michael O'Leary £350 for using too many words in that last sentence.

Pictured on Aconcagua is Liverpool supporter Mark Burley, hopefully no relation to Craig, and who has no chance of marrying Liz Hurley since she announced she favours double-barreled surnames.

Mark is from Ascot, but ditched the traditional clothing etiquette of top-hat and tails for a Liverpool shirt and hat as he took the Kop Summer Challenge 5 at Camp 2, which makes a change from the five-fingered salutes we get from Camp Nou.

Should you be thinking of going mountaineering then don't get ripped off buying a guide-book. What else is it going to say in it other than 'go up?'

IT'S something of a mystery to us as to why the Boston Red Sox aren't called the Boston Red Socks.

We've asked everyone for an explanation, including former Liverpool left-back Julian Dix, but no-one seems to know, although it does explain why they call F1 races the Grand Prix.

It didn't take long after John W Henry bought Liverpool F Club for us to receive a Kop Summer Challenge 5 entry from Fenway Park and it was Kopite Paul Storey who got there first.

He didn't get to see a game because Fenway was covered in snow and the Red Sox are on a winter break, but it was a cracking pitcher nonetheless.

Fenway Park is located at 4 Yawkey Way in Boston, which isn't good news for your windows if you live at number 2 Yawkey Way, although not as bad as if you go out with a Red Sox fan and she won't let you past first base.

We'd like to thank a Mr R Keys for some of the material used in that last sentence.

COULD this be where Rafa Benitez signed Maxi Rodriguez from?

It's widely reported that the Argentine international arrived from Atletico Madrid for £1.5 million, but this shop in Switzerland clearly had him available at a discount.

Kop Season Ticket Holder Karen Smith was in Geneva for her Mum Lillian's 60th birthday when she spotted Maxi Discount – so called because he can get you seven goals for the price of three games – and gave a five-fingered salute in front of it.

Karen also took the Kop Summer Challenge 5 in front of Jet d'Eau, which is that fountain behind her and not the budget airline she flew there on. It's believed that Ryanair fly directly through the fountain to save on plane washing fees.

Of course Switzerland is famous for the Swiss Army Knife, although the Swiss Army are no longer able to take them abroad due to airport security restrictions.

Airport security is so strict now that only last week we heard of a Kopite who had his bladder removed at John Lennon International because it contained more than 100ml of liquid, a clear case of them taking the p*ss. Next time he'll ensure he carries it in a clear plastic bag.

After setting off security alarms on the way back from Gelsenkirchen, Wayne Rooney was forced to undergo a full body search, although for once he didn't have to pay for it.

THE Azure Window in Gozo is so called because like all windows, particularly those belonging to shops on Tottenham High Road, it won't be in place forever.

It was created thousands of years ago when two limestone caves collapsed but is now said to be crumbling away and could completely disappear in the coming years. But that's enough about Goodison Park, back to The Azure Window.

A popular tourist landmark, it is often described as being 'table-like' and Fat Frank Lampard Junior was considering hiring it as the top table at his wedding until he realised it needed to be big enough for Christine Bleakley and other family members to sit at as well.

Berlin-based Red Steve Oakes, who originally comes from the Welsh town of Penmaenmawr and will be the only Kop reader who knows if we've spelt it right, visited Gozo this summer and took the Kop Summer Challenge 5 in front of the Azure Window.

Gary Neville owns a villa on Gozo, but is so ugly that when he first went to visit the Azure Window they shut the curtains.

WE'VE heard of Americans visiting Liverpool to see the Super Lamb Bananas, but not of a Super Lamb Banana visiting America to take the Kop Summer Challenge 5.

That's all changed after this SLB visited the Southernmost point in continental USA, Key West, no relation to Kanye, John, Colin, Fred or Rose.

The Super Lamb Banana, which presumably you have to peel wool off to eat, was joined in Florida by Liverpool supporters Cath Reeves, Laura Frain and Kate Palmer, who gave five-fingered salutes in front of the giant concrete buoy that marks the spot.

As well as Key West, Florida is also famous for its contribution to woodwork (the Miami Vice), a famous flower show (Orlando Bloom) and a leprechaun funded by Manchester United fans (Malcolm Glazer).

A report in 2010 revealed that the Glazers had taken £22.9 million out of United in fees and loans, something the club's supporters failed to stop them doing by wearing green and gold scarves for a few months.

They also opted not to protest against Fergie despite him taking £28.1 million out of the club and giving it to Lazio for Juan Sebastian Veron.

Barcelona have also taken something out of United – the p*ss.

WHEN Finland-based Red Vesa Vares told us he'd taken the Kop Summer Challenge 5 in Statue Park we wondered how on earth he'd managed to get on the pitch when Liverpool were man-marking from a set piece.

Turns out he was referring to Statue Park in Budapest, Hungary, where a collection of monuments from a repulsive tyranny are situated, much like in the Old Trafford museum.

Apparently the statues give an impression of what Budapest was like under communist rule, although quite why

there's one of Andy Carroll running with Mike Ashley's handkerchief in his left hand we've no idea.

Before owning Sports Direct and Newcastle United, Ashley ran a used communist cars business but it went bust after they kept Stalin. It's also believed that the principles of Communism were formed in Newcastle as it is largely regarded as being a classless society.

In contrast, former Liverpool boss Rafa Benitez has always been against communism and it's been well documented that he rejected Marxism in favour of zonal marking.

Vesa gave five-fingered salutes in front of three statues, one of which depicts a giant pair of hands catching a ball. It's believed the sculptor had never seen Jim

Leighton keep goal.

The other picture shows Hungarian communist leader Bela Kun marshalling the masses and we recently discovered that back in the USSR the dictator reported to Lenin, but not McCartney.

THE Kop has been to a lot of places since the Summer Challenge 5 started, but the North-South Korean border is a new one for us.

Called the Demilitarized zone – aka the DMZ – it is the most heavily fortified border in the world, although this is expected to change the next time anyone from the Dalglish family asks him a perfectly innocent question.

Manchester United fans sing 'you eat dogs in your home country' to their South Korean international Ji-Sung Park, which is quite ironic as they usually marry them. Or their cousins.

Liverpool supporters Ben and Lorraine Armstrong, from Lunt Village near Thornton, and Kiki, from China, took The Kop Summer Challenge 5 south of the border,

although there was no sign of Oliver Stone.

North Korea is a secretive state and its leader Kim Jong-Il is said to be a master of propaganda and social manipulation who has brainwashed his people into thinking he is almost God-like.

Of course nobody outside North Korea believes his nonsense, although we'd like to take this opportunity to congratulate his highness on his round of 38 under par featuring five holes-in-one during his first round of golf in 1994.

Thankfully you won't find such a manipulative, self-deluded, big-headed, drivel-spouting dictator who believes the world is conspiring against him in England.

He now manages Real Madrid.

HAVING won the Premier League at Blackburn, Wayne Rooney had '19' shaved onto his chest and posted the picture on Twitter.

Many people assumed he did so to taunt Liverpool supporters because the Mancs had won a 19th league title, but in truth it was so every time he looks in the mirror he can see the number 91 – his favourite age for a woman.

Ryan Giggs also shaved a message into his chest, but we're not allowed to tell you what it said.

Alex Ferguson tried to take out a super-injunction to prevent the media revealing details of an embarrassing affair, but the judge ruled that everyone could

report that he paid £7.4 million for Bebe.

Kopite Matty Holmes – not to be confused with the former West Ham footballer who almost had to have his leg amputated after a challenge from Kevin Muscat – decided he couldn't let Rooney get away without a response, so here it is.

The Southport-based Red isn't blessed with the same amount of chest hair as Rooney, or indeed a 91-year-old woman, so used pieces of tape to remind the former Everton badge kisser of who rules the Roost when it comes to European Cups.

We can also reveal that Gary Neville was going to shave '19' into his muzzie, but had to abandon his plans as it won't be grown until 2062.

Summer CHALLENGE

LAS Vegas is one of those places where it's incredibly easy to gamble a lot of your money with little hope of any tangible return. Another is Bangkok, but only if you're in a meeting with Bryan Robson.

Despite the vast amount of money swimming around in Vegas it's not a place Premier League managers often visit, although it's believed that Rafa Benitez used a roulette wheel to pick his teams for League Cup matches.

Kopite Steven Lee took the Kop Summer Challenge 5 in Vegas this summer and revealed through his choice of clothing what his strategy was when it came to roulette – always bet on charcoal.

Steven gave his five-fingered salute in front of a boat, the Statue of Liberty, a roller-coaster and several skyscrapers – all of which Mohamed Al Fayed is planning to build outside Craven Cottage over the next five years.

Stretching 4.2 miles, 'The Strip' in Vegas is the second longest strip in the world. The first is the one Peter Crouch wears at Tottenham.

Vegas is also known as Sin City, although at least the casinos there promote healthy eating by having thousands of fruit machines available.

BOB Marley remains Jamaica's biggest icon despite Robbie Earle having played for them in the World Cup.

The singer-songwriter's music has inspired millions while his hairstyle was later copied by former Sheffield Wednesday winger Reggae Blinker. Rafa Benitez was considering growing dreadlocks to go with his goatee a few years back but decided against it as he's not a rafafarian.

Even admitting that he shot the sheriff (he denied killing his deputy) failed to dilute Bob's popularity and you can now go on Bob Marley tours, which Kopite Stuart Taylor did.

Not only did he take The Kop Summer Challenge 5 in the Bob Marley Museum, Stuart also gave a five-fingered salute on Marley's actual bed in Nine Miles, Jamaica, with girlfriend Amanda Bishop. Had Amanda not been there Stuart would have been advised not to cry.

It was in that very room where Marley was inspired to write 'Get Up Stand Up' as that's how his mum woke him up before school every morning.

Stuart also took The Kop Summer Challenge 5 in Jamaica's Official Bobsleigh shop at Montego Bay Airport, a place that pays homage to the Jamaican Bobsleigh team that debuted at the 1988 Winter Olympics and had their exploits turned into a film called Cool Runnings.

There are plans afoot to make a film about the life-story of a former Liverpool player. We can't reveal who it is yet but the working title is 'Kewell Limpings'.

IF John W Henry was wondering why there were a total of 12,000 empty seats inside Anfield for the Wolves and Bolton games last Christmas he should have come to us for the answer: everyone was in Australia.

Upper Centenary Season Ticket holder Darren Watson was another Red to go down under for the cricket and he persuaded one of England's top cricketers to take the Kop Summer Challenge 5 with him.

Step forward Ian Bell – although not too far as you'll end up getting stumped, unless one of Arsenal's goalkeepers happens to be keeping wicket.

The Warwickshire batsman was on Coventry's books as a youngster and supports Aston Villa, but he put that awful childhood behind him to give five-fingered salute.

Gerard Houllier's former side largely had a terrible 2010/11 and Villa fans are revolting. They're also unhappy with who their new manager is.

BRUGES are best remembered for being Liverpool's opponents in the 1978 European Cup final at Wembley, but it shouldn't be forgotten that the Reds also won the UEFA Cup in the Belgian city in 1973, or nineshteenshseventyshthree as it was pronounced by travelling Kopites after a night on the Stella.

In April the Belgian brewer launched their first ever cider product, Stella Cidre, with a marketing campaign that reminds customers c'est cidre, not cider. We'd like to remind you all that Marouane Fellaini is a wankre.

Such has been the demand for Stella Cidre that the brewer they were running out of Jonagold apples, making it the biggest apple crisis since Eve ate one in the Garden of Eden. Adam had his eyes on a nice pear.

Bruges attracts a fair number of tourists wishing to sample its alcoholic delights and amongst them were Kopites Jamie Fisher (centre), his brother Andrew (right) and Rocko, aka Septic Tank (left).

The lads managed to take time out from their busy elbow-bending session to raise five fingers to Liverpool's European Cup successes at De Rozenhoedkaai (Quai of the Rosary) - the most photographed spot in Bruges.

Damien Comolli should be sponsored by Stella Artois. All the players he signs are reassuringly expensive.

EVEN though it took place almost 130 years ago, the Gunfight at the O.K. Corral remains regarded as the most famous gunfight in the Wild West.

The three Earp brothers and Doc Holliday took on the Clantons, McLaurys and Billy Claiborne with only three men killed despite 30 shots being fired in 30 seconds – the worst strike rate until Carlton Cole became a professional footballer.

Kopite Marty Harding took the Kop Summer Challenge 5 outside the O.K. Corral in Tombstone, Arizona, although these days it's more dangerous to do so in the O.L.D. Swan, Liverpool.

Marty's wife Sharon was behind the camera and she also snapped him giving a five-fingered salute with the Georgia Harley-Davidson riders, who were biking through Arizona.

David Beckham bought a Harley while in America and he was stopped by a police officer for driving too slowly. "The sign said 21," said Goldenbrains, only for the officer to respond: "That's the Interstate number, not the speed limit."

The officer then spotted Posh Spice looking white as a sheet and throwing up by the side of the road. "What's up with her?" he enquired.

"I'm not sure," replied Beckham, "She's been like that ever since we went down Interstate 205."

2011 shorts

The 2-1 win against Bolton on New Year's day was the first time Liverpool have won a Premier League game after conceding the first goal since the 3-2 win over Bolton in August 2009

Steven Gerrard made his 550th appearance for the club against Blackburn in January, becoming only the 10th player to do so, but also missed his 7th penalty, the same number as Billy Liddell

Jay Spearing made his first start in a Premier League game at Anfield against Everton in what was the first Merseyside derby neither Steven Gerrard or Jamie Carragher have played in since February 2002

The 3-0 win at Wolves was Kenny Dalglish's first as LFC manager since a 3-1 victory over Everton on Feb 9, 1991 and his first away league win since a 1-0 success at Coventry in November 1990

John Pantsil's own goal in the Fulham game was the first to give Liverpool a 1-0 win at Anfield since Aston Villa's Mark Delaney put through his own net in 2004

Lucas made his 100th Premier League appearance against Wigan in February, becoming the 162nd player to appear 100 times in the league for the club

9,394 days after first being appointed as Liverpool manager, Kenny Dalglish managed Liverpool for the first time in Europe when the Reds faced Sparta Prague

Liverpool's 3-1 win against Man United in March meant the Reds had beaten them three times in a row at Anfield for the first time since winning seven on the bounce between 1972-1979

Pepe Reina made his 300th appearance for Liverpool against SC Braga, becoming only the 6th goalkeeper to do so for the club

Dirk Kuyt's goal at Sunderland ensured his goal tally reached double figures for the 5th consecutive season

Kop Barfly quiz of the year

1. Who was the last player to score at Anfield under Roy Hodgson?
2. When Kenny Dalglish got the call from John W Henry to become the club's manager again he was enjoying a holiday through which cruise ship company?
3. Who made his final appearance for Liverpool in Howard Webb's 1-0 FA Cup victory against us in January?
4. On a manic January transfer deadline day, which player did Liverpool sign on loan as well as buying Luis Suarez and Andy Carroll?
5. Who was the only player to score a goal in European competition for Liverpool in 2011?
6. Which Liverpool player scored against his former club in March?
7. Which two players were sent off in the Under-18s FA Youth Cup exit to Manchester United at Anfield?
8. What shirt number did Andy Carroll wear in the Europa League?
9. Raul Meireles scored his last Liverpool goal against which side?
10. Who made his Liverpool debut against Manchester City in April?
11. Which player conceded penalties in back-to-back appearances in March/April?
12. Who scored seven goals in three games in April/May?
13. Who was the only outfield player start every game under Dalglish in 2010/11?
14. Which player sat on the bench for the first time in the Premier League on the final day of the 2010/121season?
15. Who scored our first goal of pre-season 2011/12?
16. Which Liverpool player played against Liverpool in a pre-season match?
17. Who gave up the number 26 shirt so Charlie Adam could wear it?

18. Which fixture saw both Andy Carroll and Luis Suarez score in the same game for the first time?
19. Which club did Nabil el Zhar sign for?
20. Before Luis Suarez against Sunderland, who was the last Liverpool player to miss a penalty at Anfield?

 **footage of the year**

LIVERPOOL supporters celebrate Dirk Kuyt's hat-trick clinching goal against the Mancs in Harry's Bar, Singapore. The place is buzzing so much you'd think it was the King Harry.

http://www.youtube.com/watch?v=6hwS7ERcMNs

THE travelling Kop give Steve Bruce's head and the Suarez song an airing in a Stadium of Light concourse. The Suarez bounce, anyone?

http://www.youtube.com/watch?v=ie6dGxFdLqc&feature=related (or search for Suarez song Sunderland)

Mr K Dalglish, Anfield L4

Licensed to win silverware, serve doubles and trebles and to provide champagne football

Answers

1. Joe Cole
2. Silveresa
3. Ryan Babel
4. Conor Thomas
5. Dirk Kuyt
6. Glen Johnson (v West Ham)
7. Stephen Sama & Conor Coady
8. 29 (as Torres had worn 9 previously)
9. Wigan Athletic
10. Jon Flanagan
11. Soto Kyrgiakos
12. Maxi Rodriguez
13. Dirk Kuyt
14. Andre Wisdom
15. Christian Poulsen
16. Peter Gulacsi (for Hull)
17. Jay Spearing
18. Exeter away
19. Levante
20. Joe Cole (v Trabzonspor)
21. Martin Skrtel, Charlie Adam
22. Reading (2006)
23. Mike Jones
24. Newcastle (Feb 2007)
25. Steve Nicol, Dominic Matteo, Gary McAllister

21. Who scored their first goals at the Kop end in August?
22. Before the game at Exeter, who were Liverpool's opponents the last time Pepe Reina appeared in a League Cup game?
23. Which referee sent off two players in the 4-0 defeat at Spurs?

24. Before his goal at Brighton, against which club did Craig Bellamy score his last goal in domestic football for Liverpool?
25. Charlie Adam is one of only four Scottish-born players to score Premier League goals for Liverpool. Can you name the other three?

2011 shorts

When Liverpool faced West Brom in April it was the first time they had met a side managed by someone who had also managed the Reds in the same season since playing David Ashworth's Oldham in December 1922

Andy Carroll scored his first goals for Liverpool against Man City and his first goals at Anfield on the day he started up front with Luis Suarez for the first time in a home game

The 5-0 win against Birmingham meant that Liverpool have scored four or more goals in a league game for 85 successive seasons – an English record

Jamie Carragher made his 666th appearance for the club against Fulham, taking him to second place in LFC's all-time appearance list

By netting at Fulham, Dirk Kuyt became the first player to score in five consecutive league games since John Aldridge in March 1989

Against Aston Villa, Martin Skrtel became one of only two outfield players to play in every minute of every Premier League game in 2010/12

The attendance of 45,018 against Sunderland in August was a new Anfield Premier League record, beating the 44,983 that attended the Spurs game in 2006

Liverpool's 2-0 win at The Emirates was their biggest away win at Arsenal since a 2-0 victory in September 1983

Charlie Adam, Andy Carroll, Stewart Downing, Jon Flanagan, Jordan Henderson, Raul Meireles, Jack Robinson, Maxi Rodriguez and Luis Suarez made their League Cup debuts at Exeter

The 0-4 defeat at Spurs saw two Liverpool players sent off in the same game for the 6th time

Liverpool became the first side to win at Brighton's AMEX Stadium

PEPE Reina does a spot of singing his way live on a Spanish TV show. How come you never see Tim Howard on Letterman?

http://www.youtube.com/watch?v=vcznNNn9JTY

The Kop mourns the death of Bill Shankly at the Oulu Palloseura game in 1981.

http://www.youtube.com/watch?v=LGgg9HHlz3c

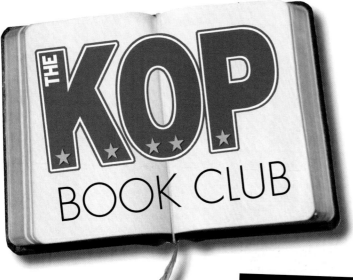

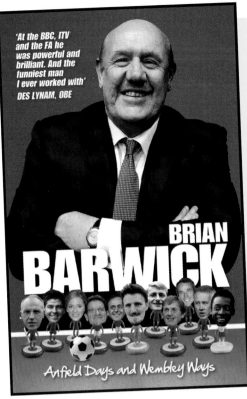

'At the BBC, ITV and the FA he was powerful and brilliant. And the funniest man I ever worked with'
DES LYNAM, OBE

BRIAN BARWICK
Anfield Days and Wembley Ways

BRIAN BARWICK has enjoyed the most amazing life in and around football.

He has had the privilege of rubbing shoulders with countless legends and held some of the biggest jobs in the game... from Chief Executive of the FA to Editor of Match of the Day.

This is a remarkable journey from the terraces of Anfield to the corridors of power at Soho Square.

Barwick oversaw the completion of the new Wembley stadium and went on to hire Capello – and McClaren - before leaving for his next adventure.

Throughout it all, he never lost his passion for the Reds. Growing up with greats like Shankly, Paisley and 'Sir' Roger Hunt saw to that.

This is a warm, witty and sometimes poignant tale of a footy-mad Kopite who climbed to the top of the soccer ladder.

Sale Price £12.99
KOP 20 Price £10.39
+ £2 P&P (UK)

New updated edition
ALRIGHT ALDO SOUND AS A POUND
On the road with everybody's favourite Irish Scouser

ALDO - aka John Aldridge - is the former Liverpool Football Club striking legend who travels all over Europe following the fortunes of his beloved reds during his media work.

In 'Alright Aldo' - the updated paperback version no less - the proud Irish Scouser draws on years of experience to produce a book that is full of hilarious inside stories.

From Anfield to Dublin, Newport to the Mexico World Cup and Istanbul to Cardiff, Aldo relives the funny side of being a professional footballer and what it's like working on the other side as one of the media.

It's a journey that you won't want to miss!

Sale Price £6.99
KOP 20 Price £5.59
+ £2 P&P (UK)

BILL SHANKLY is one of the greatest figures in football. His only authorised autobiography was a best-seller in the 1970s and is now available in paperback and as an eBook.

Ghost-written by John Roberts - one of the only journalists Shankly trusted to tell his life story - this is the tale of his rise from a poor Scottish mining village to international fame as creator of the most successful side of the era - Liverpool.

Written in the years after his dramatic resignation as Liverpool manager, it gives an insight into Shankly's feelings about the club that he felt had turned its back on him, and explores the astonishing relationship he had with the supporters they called 'Shankly's Red Army'.

Sale Price £6.99
KOP 20 Price £5.59 + £2 P&P (UK)

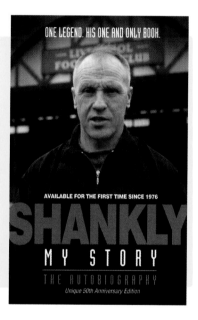

ONE LEGEND. HIS ONE AND ONLY BOOK.
AVAILABLE FOR THE FIRST TIME SINCE 1976
SHANKLY
MY STORY
THE AUTOBIOGRAPHY
Unique 50th Anniversary Edition

'Geoff proved time and time again, as you will see in this book, there was no better judge of talent in the English game' - Alan Hansen

SECRET DIARY of a LIVERPOOL SCOUT

Stories behind the signings that shaped football history

SIMON HUGHES

FEW people know about the major role played behind the scenes by Geoff Twentyman, the club's chief scout from 1959 to 1984.

A former Anfield player, Twentyman was recruited into the bootroom team by Bill Shankly and went on to unearth a host of world-famous stars that helped to maintain the Reds' position as one of Europe's greatest teams during a glittering era.

Twentyman worked tirelessly, travelling up and down the country in his trademark Cortina to write reports on young up-and-coming professionals such as Alan Hansen, Terry McDermott, Steve Nicol and Ian Rush. Twentyman casts his expert eye over young hopefuls that were to become legends of the game as well as others that failed to make the top grade.

Sale Price £6.99
KOP 20 Price £5.59 + £2 P&P (UK)

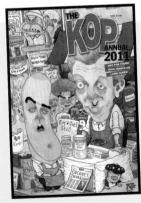

THE KOP ANNUAL 2011

LIKE a Roy Hodgson away win, The Kop Annual comes around once a year.

Despite the cockney invasion, there was still plenty to have a laugh about in our 2011 edition, including spotting the difference between Pepe Reina's head and Jimmy Hill's chin...

Sale Price £2
KOP 20 Price £1.60
+ £1 P&P (UK)

THE KOP BOOK CLUB

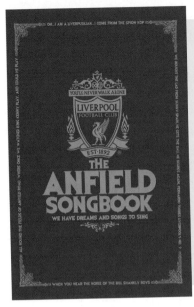

ANFIELD is a place of worship. And when it comes to inventing funny and inspirational songs for their team. No other set of fans can compare with the famous Kopites of Liverpool Football Club.

The Anfield Songbook is a collection of the timeless anthems, traditional classics, player chants and witty one-liners that have made the Kop unique.

Merseyshop Price £9.99
KOP 20 Price £7.99
FREE P&P (UK)

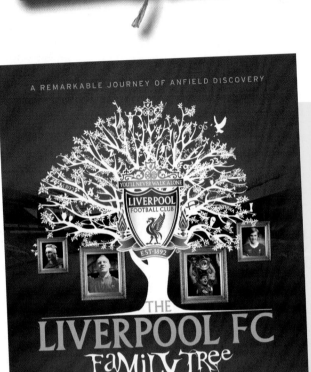

A REMARKABLE JOURNEY OF ANFIELD DISCOVERY

THE LIVERPOOL FC FAMILY TREE

FOREWORD BY KENNY DALGLISH

EVER wondered what goes to make up a special club like Liverpool FC?

Our Anfield family roots provide the answer.

From the small Scottish mining village that was Shankly's birthplace to Hetton-le-Hole, the home town of the club's most successful manager, Bob Paisley.....

......from the Bootle playing fields where Jamie Carragher learned his trade to the medieval Finnish town that gave birth to Sami Hyypia..........

The magic of Liverpool FC is made up of may different people and places.

This book takes you on a colourful journey of discovery - through eight unique excursions linking the Anfield past and present.

The Liverpool Family Tree is the most unusual and revealing story of a football club you'll ever read.

It is guaranteed to unearth some fascinating secrets about your LFC loved ones that even the most ardent of supporters have yet to discover.

Just like researching your own family, this book will inspire you, make you laugh, provoke emotion and ultimately fill you with pride.

Merseyshop Price £16.99
KOP 20 Price £13.59 - FREE P&P (UK)

A LIVERPOOL team without Steven Gerrard and Jamie Carragher in it seems unthinkable.

This 84-page special edition celebrates their careers of Stevie and Carra, and is packed with great images, tributes, stats and even quizzes, and is an essential addition to any Liverpool FC fan's reading collection.

Merseyshop Price £3.99
KOP 20 Price £3.19
+£1 P&P (UK)

CELEBRATE Kenny Dalglish's second coming and revisit the career of arguably the finest player to pull on a red shirt.

It is packed with classic archive images as well as insight and revealing stories from the great man himself.

A must for Reds young and old.

Merseyshop Price £3.99
KOP 20 Price £3.19
+£1 P&P (UK)

Call 0845 143 0001 or visit www.merseyshop.com

Prices subject to change. Please enquire for overseas postage.

Now sign up for a year of Kop laughs

If you like what you've read, why not subscribe to The Kop magazine every month of the year? We like taking the mick out of ourselves, but love having a laugh at our rivals' expense even more . . .

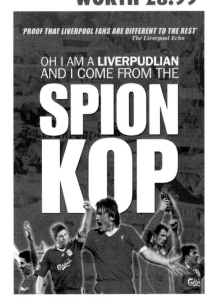

FREE
WORTH £8.99

'PROOF THAT LIVERPOOL FANS ARE DIFFERENT TO THE REST'
The Liverpool Echo

OH I AM A **LIVERPUDLIAN** AND I COME FROM THE

SPION KOP

Get a FREE copy of SPION KOP when you subscribe to The Kop Magazine. Simply quote KOPSK when ordering – NO JOKE!

THE Kop Annual is just a flavour of what is produced every month in The Kop magazine.

So if you enjoy reading about the serious Anfield issues, but also love poking fun at the Mancs and falling about laughing at Everton's latest clanger, why not sign up for a year's supply of The Kop?

Just call us on 0845 143 0001 or you can also visit merseyshop.com.

Or take a look at our yearly rates, fill in the form below and send it to Kop Subscriptions, Sport Media, PO Box 48, Old Hall Street, Liverpool L69 3EB.

Sign up for The Kop – it'll have you laughing more than John W Henry walking into a bank with £50million in his pocket.

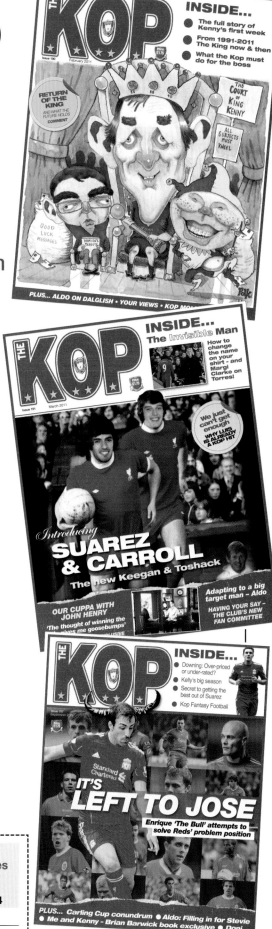

YOUR DETAILS

Mr/Mrs/Ms: ____ Initial: __ Surname: _____

Address: _____

_____ Zip/postcode: _____ Country: _____

Tel no: _____ Email: _____ Date of birth: _____

☐ I enclose a cheque/postal order for £ ☐ made payable to SPORT MEDIA

KOP yearly subscription prices
UK £24
Europe £31.44
Rest of world £37.44

Alternatively, call 0845 143 0001 or log on to www.merseyshop.com

HEY LOOK, THAT GUY'S THROWING A BOTTLE ONTO THE PITCH!
IT'S OK. WE QUITE OFTEN LOSE OUR BOTTLE AGAINST THESE
DO YOU THINK THEY WILL ADD THIS GAME TO THE STADIUM TIMELINE?
PHEW. TURNED AWAY JUST IN TIME
IT'S ENOUGH TO TAKE THE HAIRS OFF YER CHEST
WHAT A JOLLY WELL TAKEN GOAL BY A FINE PLAYER
MAKE MINE A BITTER
I'M GLAD I BROUGHT ME DARK GLASSES
WHAT A WASTE OF...
WINSLOW HERE I COME
THIS CALLS FOR A LITTLE LIE-DOWN